The Other Side of the Ribbon

The Other Side of the Ribbon

A scrapbook of eccentric adventures
in local newspaper offices

Written and drawn by
Brian Thomas

This book is dedicated to the late respected journalist Lance Samson, a man of kindness and good counsel who left this world far too soon. He kept me sharp and on my toes and, through good and bad times (often driving each other to distraction), we never lost an inner respect for each other. He would surely have laughed heartily at many of these memories.

Also to my first chief reporter, the late Noel Wain, whose tinder-dry wit guided me through my fledgling times as a reporter on the *Falmouth Packet*.

To the incomparable Sue Geatches who made her resident trainee days so much fun with her irrepressible sense of the ridiculous.

And to writer/reporter Mike Truscott, who continues to dispense sage advice and granular humour to a fellow retired scribe.

Also, RIP to three fine men who left us in 2015. Retired *Mid-Devon Advertiser* former chief photographer Rex Hitchcock, whose deprecating humour and consistent pessimism made the working day much easier to bear and whose innate camera skills and incisive eye gave his pictures a special identity; his masterfully talented and shrewdly funny predecessor Arthur Kay; and likewise to my first editor, the redoubtable Roy Standring whose declamatory voice and pithy comments made his presence a joy.

The everyday incidents recorded herein took place during my reporting career spanning from 1974 to 1998 and are selected randomly from twenty four fascinating, funny, fulfilling and remarkably unadventurous years.

I am grateful to a panoply of wonderful, diverse colleagues (even the ones I unintentionally, and sometimes intentionally, fell out with) for their memorable contributions to generally commonplace office incidents, many of which were faithfully recorded thanks to Mr Isaac Pitman and his magic shorthand and my "bizarrely interpretative" cartoonist's eye. Almost all the names and many of the locations have been changed in order to protect the dramatis personae (including me).

Receptionist Harriet Lang enters the news room and looks around at the three occupants.

Harriet: "Has anyone got any string?"

There is a general silence except for some typing sounds, which continue. Clearly the request, if heard, is considered so low a priority that it fails to register.

Harriet (*batting on regardless*): "Or the keys to the editor's office. The string's in there."

Sub-editor Sam: "I haven't got any string, and Edwin's office is locked. He's out."

Harriet: "Who's got the key?"

Sam: "Edwin."

Harriet (*disbelievingly*): "Come on..."

Sam: "He's taken his keys with him."

Chief reporter Beeno (*remembering absent sub-editor Tom; unhelpfully suggesting*): "Tom's got a set of keys. But he's on holiday in Canada."

Harriet: "What, and taken them with him?"

Sam: "They're probably at home."

Harriet: "Oh, hell."

Sam: "Sorry."

Harriet: "This is ridiculous."

Beeno: "True."

Harriet: "What's he got in there, the Crown Jewels?"

Reporter Teebone (*quiet until now; impatiently, without looking up from his typewriter*):

"He's got string..."

Introduction

Receptionist
(peering around door of newsroom, brightly)
There's a lady in reception who wants to see
a reporter. She does a lot of work for charity.

Jaded, underpaid reporter
(without looking up, darkly)
Don't we all...

All reporters have notebooks of one kind or another, even those who employ recording devices.

They use them to make a (mostly) shorthand record of the many interviews they conduct, in person or by phone, and all the meetings and events they attend.

Over the years I have always kept a second type of record in my notebook: a journal of what goes on outside those narrow confines; that place on the opposite side of the typewriter ribbon. Not the side that carries the news to the readers, but that alternative place where the purveyors of that information wander and graze.

This colossal but claustrophobic neighbourhood comprises trivial bits of in-office silliness that bind together a bunch of disparate people in the pursuit of one vaguely-defined goal: to collect enough material to fill each edition of your local newspaper, and to do it on time and as accurately as possible without resorting to uncontained panic or advanced fisticuffs.

This is a collection of private moments, noted quickly at the time because of their delightful daftness, their heart-warming charm or their indelible frustrations; moments that express the joy (and despair) of working closely, and at the same time loosely, with others as fallible as you.

Like, for instance, the reporter giving a fascinating insight into his grasp of petrology when he announced, apparently knowledgeably, in a telephone interview with an expert geologist: "Stones are rocks, in a sense, aren't they?"

Or the reporter who rang Buckingham Palace Press office, got no immediate reply and announced to the office: "Well, I don't think Liz is at home at present... Oh, hello. I didn't think you were there for a minute."

Or, indeed, the reporter who called a local police station after hearing that a large snake was loose in their country town and during the course of the conversation reflected his paper's obsession with giving pets a family-friendly moniker by asking: "Do you know if the snake had a name?" (The reply should surely have been "Are you taking the hiss?")

One thing to be guaranteed from this book is that you will learn very little about the serious mechanics of journalism – though you may get an idea why the production of a weekly, daily or evening newspaper is most definitely a "minor miracle," as a former editor of mine once accurately described it.

It's what goes on behind the scenes – those moments of great stress, those times of spectacular discord, those days of innocent fun, the belly laughs, the sobs of delight, the aching sides – and the wonderful, unconventional and flawed humans you meet along the way that make that miracle all the more remarkable. I know. I was one of that motley band.

To quote the much-referenced Lord Thomson of Fleet: "It is part of the social mission of every great newspaper to provide a refuge and a home for the largest possible number of salaried eccentrics."

So, let us look at these curious people who produce these "minor miracles" of news coverage each week or each day. They're called an Editorial Team – though, unlike a team of athletes, they often run around in different directions falling over each other.

Perhaps their activities will remind you of the idiosyncrasies of your own work place, whatever and wherever it may be...

Helpful Guide to Terms Used Throughout

Sub – A sub-editor. Someone who "subs" (edits) copy. Not the editor, though an editor also subs pages, nor a sandwich or an undersea vessel.

Copy – The material created by reporters; their stories.

Pars – Short for "paragraphs."

Blacks – Carbon copies of typed news stories, retained in case the top copy is lost.

Spike – Reporters and subs once utilized a pointed steel rod set in a short wooden base to impale discarded material such as used (and often unused) Press releases. This was a rough filing system in case one needed to refer to the original documents again – mostly when someone rang up to point out an error in our rendition of their submitted masterpiece. The spike sat next to them on the desk, both for easy access and impending injury. A notorious sub-editor, known to fly into easily-triggered rages, once threatened to insert a spike into the palm of a printer who had annoyed him. Thankfully, it was only a threat. So, as can be expected, these lethal desk tidies proved a mite too dangerous for both the health and safety folk and individual common sense and were eventually largely eradicated. Instead we began collecting previously-impaled detritus in loose piles on shelves, until they finally fell over and were relegated to the waste bin. Or they fell on to a night storage heater and the building burned down.

Broadsheet – Large size of newspaper, approximately 29½ by 23½ inches (749mm x 597 mm) for a full spread (which is one heck of a stretch for a reader and the bane of many a commuter carriage). It is twice the size of a standard **Tabloid** (which is roughly 17 by 11 inches or 432mm x 279 mm) and tends to be less "sensational" in its reportage.

Part One
A Cornucopia of Specialists

The Editor – Sub-Editor – Reporters
Photographer – Printer – Results

A Cornucopia of Specialists

The Editor

Reporter to Editor
Why have you used "this reviewer" in your piece about the Royal Shakespeare Society instead of "I," which is considerably shorter?

Editor
I don't like the word "I."

At the top of the news room tree, there's the **Editor**.

Editors have been described as "a lonely lot, all characterised by the belief that they are, individually, the best writers/journalists in the world."

American writer/publisher Elbert Hubbard (1856-1915) famously observed that an editor was "a person employed by a newspaper, whose business it is to separate the wheat from the chaff, and to see that the chaff is   printed."

Any story ideas an editor conceives – or, indeed, any stories proposed by his or her marriage partner, friends, neighbours, intimate business acquaintances, children or pets – are the most important issues ever conceived and must be pursued at the expense of anything else, such as better stories, or even the private life, sleep patterns and general well-being of the unfortunate scribe who has been saddled with the projects.

Though you may have exhausted a huge encyclopaedia of intimate and incisive questions on the subject at hand, your cheery editor will always come up with a selection of his own questions that you may have "forgotten" to ask. Then you face the prospect of ringing back a contact and saying: "Sorry to bother you again, I just wanted to check..." And when you have the reply and take it to your editor, you are delighted to hear him say: "Ah, yes, could you ring him back and just ask him...?"

At which point you get the office chain saw and cleave his desk in half.

An especially jaded local weekly editor considers his position

It's true that editors have a lot of unenviable responsibilities – legal, administrative, attempting to control the untamed clan beneath them in the pecking order, and protecting the good name of the publication that will hopefully outlive their stewardship. This is clearly in mind in an editor's response to a query about how his newspaper seemed to be the only business in the Western hemisphere not to possess a fax machine.

"I never said I was against having a fax machine. It's just a low priority. I want to make sure we've got typewriters and toilet rolls first."

(And, as if to prove the point, there will be more on each of those important items later).

However, my point about finicky editors is illustrated by this exchange, on the cusp of a final copy deadline when space for stories is virtually non-existent.

Reporter
How many paragraphs do you want on this? Two? Four?
Editor
(*after a long think*)
Three.

An editor of a weekly paper, answering a telephone complaint, explained: "If we get something wrong, we put it right. Thank God, we don't get it wrong very often..." To which a jaundiced reporter muttered: "Only once a week..."

The Sub-Editor

The **Sub-editors** are one link down in the newsroom chain of command, though they are rarely bothered by this. They lay out pages in a corner of the news room, talking to themselves and occasionally shrieking for copy to fill an unexpected gap in their ingenious blueprints.

At one time, subs used to lay out pages using sheets of ruled paper and coloured chinagraph pencils; each finished page would be bundled up with its typed and subbed stories, paper-clipped together and sent to the printers. Now they construct their pages on a computer screen, taking reporters' work direct from their individual computers, and inserting and electronically cropping any pictures required. Disks of the assembled pages then go to the printers.

A busy day in the contemporary subbing calendar

Subs can edit a reporter's precious copy with the disrespect of a shady butcher but are occasionally useful as an alibi as you can always blame a sub for any mistakes you made in a published story. Most subs are reclusive and avoid meeting the public in the same way that bats only come out at night.

A reckless trainee once announced in the middle of the office: "One of the questions in my exam was *What are subs for?* I left it blank and still got it right." At which point the Editor looked up from his subbing duties and asked: "Do you have a death wish, Whitney?"

Sometimes subs are kind, and let you get away with a little journalistic flippancy. Sometimes they err on the side of caution – and probably save the bacon of the over-enthusiastic.

I once wrote a story about two naked men racing through a town centre and managed to get away with the *Lone Ranger* inspired line *With a flash of flesh and a hearty "Hi ho, Streaker!"*

But when a renowned local artist asked me to write a story about the birth of his first child, my opening line went a little too far and was promptly excised by the sub, for conspicuous reasons: *It took more than a couple of strokes of the brush to create John Smith's latest masterpiece.*

Subs often have a passionate devotion to duty. A colleague told me of one sub-editor who was taken ill at work and was being stretchered out by paramedics. As he reached the door he grabbed the editor's arm with a vice-like grip. "I've done page three!" he gasped dutifully, before flopping back to supine mode and being whisked off to the ambulance.

Subs are also notorious for wasting reporters' time – say, about the length of an article. They tell you "let it run," so you present them with 800 words and they mercilessly cut it to two skimpy paragraphs.

I remember a fellow reporter putting in a rather lengthy story one day to hear this exasperated exchange.

Sub
547 words?!
Reporter
It's for a single column.
Sub
I didn't ask for Nelson's column.

Subs write headlines.

Sometimes they are ambiguous: FIVE SQUATTERS IN HOT WATER.

Sometimes they're intriguing: RAIN STOPS JUMPING.

Occasionally they're exhausting: NUDIST WELFARE MAN'S MODEL WIFE FELL FOR THE CHINESE HYPNOTIST FROM THE CO-OP BACON FACTORY. (Infamous *News of the World* epic).

And now and then they suggest the obvious: COLLISION WITH BUS KNOCKED ME OUT.

But mostly their headlines are littered with excruciating alliteration and dreadful puns aimed at getting the deskbound sub through the day without impaling himself with suicidal intent on the sharp end of a cheese and pickle sandwich.

In one example, the parish priest of a small North Italian town exorcised the local football team after soccer fans complained that only ghosts could have caused the town side to lose five successive home games. The headline was: PLAYING FOR A GHOULLESS DRAW...

On a similar note, a reporter on one of my papers (who eventually took the "poacher turned gamekeeper" route by becoming a sub), concluded a story about a boys' school relocating to an allegedly haunted former mansion house with the sentence: *There is a legend that the ghost of a woman dressed in blue has sometimes been seen and also a young servant girl – but perhaps the new boys will help lay them.* Ah, those pre-sexist days...

Story time...

Whenever the rival evening newspaper arrived in the office, one sub-editor would open it up and begin reading stories aloud. Sometimes he would only chose a snippet, and then ask: "Have we got this?" This regular late afternoon occurrence became known as "Story Time" (amongst other less salubrious baptisms). Reporters always felt there was an inference that they weren't doing their job if the other paper got some kind of "scoop" that their own paper hadn't picked up on.

Feeling like they were being treated as diminutives in a schoolroom, at least one of them would often snort: "We shouldn't be following *them* around. We should be looking for stories of our own." But that often backfired in the face of the question: "Well, *where are they?*" This response usually came when the other reporters were already engaged on trivial stuff – bread and butter local weekly paper items like typing out wedding reports or the results of the jam making competition at a local fete, items often demanded by the very sub in question to fill an empty hole in a page beset with an immediate deadline.

Subs can be especially pedantic at times.

A photographer was once asked by a sub-editor where he had taken a proffered topical "filler" snow scene of a seagull perched on a street light. The photographer was pretty vague about location, saying it was just a seaside winter scene. The conversation ended with the immortal: "I can't put that in the *Teignmouth Post* if it's not Teignmouth. Someone might recognise that it's not a Teignmouth street light."

Even so, they can also offer some sagacious advice in times of crisis.

Trainee reporter (*as senior reporter comes off the phone*): "The Co-op for you. Also your girlfriend rang and your wife has just called."

Senior reporter: "Oh, right. Now, where do I start?"

Sub-editor (*in learned tones*): "Work first, mistress second, wife third."

The Reporter

Reporters comprise trainees or juniors, seniors and a chief reporter-stroke-news editor.

The **Chief Reporter** or News Editor or "Poor Sap in the Middle" or "Was there really no-one else for this bloody job?" is really just an ordinary reporter with a few extra administrative tasks who sits in that no-man's-land between the needs of an Editor and the whims of reporters who all think they could do his job better but really don't want the responsibility. It is his job to dish out the day's assignments to the reporters, which means he gets to cherry-pick his work, having suffered dire assignments under previous holders of the post.

Stories coming from chance meetings, phone calls and letters – anything unexpected – are generally referred to as "Off Diary" stories where frequent, formal meetings such as local council committees, magistrates' courts, public inquiries, etcetera, are "On Diary" stories as their predetermined date and time are noted in advance in a big office diary, customarily kept and managed by "Chiefy."

Unfortunately, there are often other "duties" that the chief can get saddled with that are especially onerous.

On one occasion when in the post I was summoned by the editor and ordered to go and find a trainee reporter who had not turned up for work at nine and was becoming notorious for her lateness. I'd spoken to her about it a few times and she'd promised to do better, but it never seemed to happen. Now the editor had had enough and handed me the address of her rented flat with the words "Go and get her! And STAY with her until she comes back with you!"

I found the building in question, a large Victorian house, one of many converted to single-room flats for students, and managed to get past the main door, which was wide open, and inside. I found the trainee's flat, on the first floor, knocked on the door, announced myself, got no reply and tried the handle. The door was unlocked and I cautiously entered a murky, curtained room calling her name.

There was a groaning sound and I perceived a figure undulating sluggishly beneath a large floral duvet rumpled across a double bed behind the door. The figure sat up slowly and the duvet fell away to reveal a pretty blonde with dishevelled hair and bleary eyes staring at me with a distant, half-dreamy expression, two fulsome breasts in full view fighting to escape from the fragile confines of a flimsy nightdress. I had never felt so embarrassed, and so much like a potential sex offender on the prowl, so I quickly babbled: "Hi, Rose," [not her real name] "it's Brian. The editor sent me to get you because you didn't turn up for work and we were concerned you might be ill..." [kindly lie].

Rose dragged herself out of bed, apologised for being late as she'd been burning the candle at both ends again and started to drag some clothes on. I quickly looked away, relieved that she hadn't screamed "intruder!" or "rape!" or "police!" and that she hadn't been sharing her bed with a seven foot rock climber with an attitude problem, and decided to say to hell with the editor's demand that I STAY there and watch the poor lass dressing. "I'll be outside," I said, adding: "It's OK, take your time" and hoping she wouldn't take that literally and slip back into bed. Fortunately, she didn't, I drove her to work, the editor "had words" with her and she was late again the next day. This time I stayed at my desk.

Senior Reporters – which, of course, include the chief one – are always the worst-paid and most downtrodden folk in the working world, as their profession constantly appears at the bottom of league tables listing workers' pay and conditions, often just above lavatory cleaners, which is hardly the romantic image of a super-sleuth news hound. These are the folk you most often see at some uneventful public meeting, sitting in the corner on an uncomfortable stool, scribing away with periodic interest but mostly looking like they would rather be at home mowing the lawn.

One long-serving receptionist and Jill-of-all-trades once told me that amongst her many office duties she even had occasion to stitch up reporters' clothes when they got too ragged, thus providing sewing skills for the wretched as well as a friendly shoulder to weep on.

HAPLESS, THREADBARE REPORTER (same as today)

Here, let me sew that on for you...

Oh, and many of us are really not **hacks**. Unfortunately, the word "hack" is often employed in a rather derogatory way to describe a journalist. But what is this word hack? Well, it's to cut or notch something. It's a grated frame for drying fish. In football it is used to describe the kicking of the ball (or another player). It's coughing in a short dry manner. It's a digging tool (such as a pick), the board on which a falcon's meat is served or the state of partial liberty in which a young hawk is kept before training. Add the word "saw" and you can start cutting timber; add "watch" and it becomes a timepiece used for nautical observations.

Brewers Dictionary of Phrase and Fable says "hack" is: "Short for hackney, a horse let out for hire; hence, one whose services are for hire, especially a literary drudge, compiler, furbisher-up of other men's work." The *Longman Concise Dictionary* is even more incisive: "One who produces mediocre work for financial gain." And another dictionary adds: "Much used or worn, like a hired out horse."

Which conjures up the historic image of a reporter – a male one at least; the women are much trendier, more fragrant, and often brighter – as a rather rumpled, damaged person, loitering on a rainy street corner wearing a threadbare suit, wrinkled mackintosh and a haunted expression. He is clutching a cheap biro and a damp shorthand notebook and awaiting the arrival of some currently-fashionable celebrity to hopefully snatch some savoury comments for an impatient editor and a ravenous readership – eventually writing his tale with a host of hackneyed and trite phrases.

Hack and Hackette.
*Yes, the sign in the hat band reads DE**PRESS**ED...*
Plus fragrant alternative

As I said, we're not all like that, and I have (thankfully) met very few who reflect that popular cliché. Perhaps I've just moved in the wrong circles...

One old colleague of mine did tend to look a little careworn, a touch hedge-dragged and rather unenthusiastic and beleaguered, rather like the legendary American TV cop Columbo. But, like the fictional detective, he was exceptionally good at throwing competitors off the scent; especially if he'd grabbed a "scoop" or a particularly juicy piece of copy from a meeting. He'd often sit gazing into space, occasionally scribbling a few lines in biro on to the crumpled back page of a sub-committee agenda. At the end of the meeting/court hearing/tribunal, he'd adopt one of his most demoralized expressions, shake his head and wheeze: "There's not a LINE in it, old chap." But a couple of days later reams of copy would appear in his newspaper on the meeting/court hearing/tribunal he'd attended – and considering a ream is 500 sheets, you get the drift!

We now move on to **Trainee reporters** – once the often-unappreciated backbone of many smaller papers, employed largely because they are cheap and willing work horses. Many aspire to better things, and often go on to achieve much in a wide range of media positions. A one-time Camborne and Redruth Packet junior scribe became a columnist to the stars in California after a spell on the *New York Times*. And a former Devon & Cornwall Newspapers trainee became an internationally-renowned thriller writer after a stint with *The Times* in Hong Kong – thus defying the acerbic observation that "every journalist has a novel in him, which is an excellent place for it" [Russell Lynes, 1910-1991, former *Harper's Magazine* managing editor].

The learning curve to these golden goals is always paved with confusion.

One trainee looked up from a Press release with a frown and said: "You've got some weird names in Devon. Who's this person *J. Lamble Hontrez*? Is he Spanish?" It turned out to be J. Lamble, comma, Hon Treas – i.e. the honorary treasurer of a local organisation.

Another trainee arrived in the temperate West Country fresh-faced from the wild North and was soon puzzling over a Press release about a charity duck race. When we explained that the race involved betting on little plastic ducks with numbers on them dropped into the river, floating with the tide to a predetermined spot and retrieved with a net, he replied: "Oh. I thought it was real ducks. I was wondering how they'd get them all to go the same way..."

A new female trainee took a call in the office in the 1980s from a member of the Baha'i faith, Iranian-established Shia Muslims, whose representative wanted a little general publicity for their local group. During the interview the trainee found herself unwittingly facing a loud and rather unspiritual dressing down over a serious breach in religious etiquette, from which came the valuable lesson: think about who you are talking to before you ask a question, even if it's the same question you ask everyone.

Specifically: Don't brightly ask a follower of Islam "And what's your Christian name?"

Keen trainee duck-fancier prepares to take down a story being dictated by phone, imprecisely donning his copy-taking headset

Most of the female trainees I've worked with have been blessed with a great sense of humour. One, with a particularly wicked glint in her eye, also had a predilection for wearing very tight slacks. Legend has it that one day she was standing at a bar wearing an especially spectacular second skin when a male business contact asked her: "How on *earth* do you get into those pants?" To which she replied, without a beat: "You could start with a gin and tonic."

One trainee described himself as a "closet punk," though he always dressed pretty conventionally, so it must have been a very tiny closet. When I heard he was going to cover the formal lunch of a local hoteliers group, I couldn't resist the drawing below with the caption "Our resident closet punk prepares for upcoming Hoteliers lunch..."

The Photographer

Despite a contemporary cost-saving increase in the use of submitted snaps from readers, "citizen journalists" and reporters armed with their own cameras, you can still find a dedicated **Press Photographer** or two.

These characters are even more disgruntled than reporters and claim even worse treatment by the Establishment in terms of long hours, low pay and fragile, outdated gear. As one staff photographer dolefully told me some years back: "You can always tell our company's photographic equipment: it's the stuff with Sellotape on it."

These are the sorry souls who are sent to isolated places on rainy winter nights to capture a line-up of principals in a draughty parish hall to publicise a forthcoming village pantomime. If you see a local Press photographer in such circumstances, remember that they respond well to a *very swift* and trouble-free assignment, along with a hot cup of tea and a chocolate Garibaldi.

I have a copy of a lovely photo from a village pantomime rehearsal photo-call taken by one of my lens-wielding friends, which made it to the "funnies" board in the dark room. The impromptu "grab shot" shows an elderly lady dressed as a dwarf and wearing a huge white beard. Apparently remonstrating with another lady sitting in a plastic chair in an overcoat and beret, she is clutching her beard to her chest and gesticulating with her left hand in seemingly righteous indignation. The caption bubble reads: "So, I said to Snow White *Sod the mines, today...*"

Happy snappers on their eager way to anywhere but on an assignment

One photographer I knew had a fondness for an over-the-heads perspective and would often arrive at an outdoor assignment – certainly those involving crowds – carrying an aluminium stepladder; or, if that had been forgotten, she would disappear and reappear either hanging precariously from a lamp post or a cooperative resident's upstairs balcony. I never saw this myself, but was assured it was true. And, considering some of the antics of local press photographers that I did see, it's more than a little possible.

Another beefy lens man – (this tale may be apocryphal, but I have been assured it is not) – is alleged to have embarrassed himself and everyone else at the grand opening of a large exhibition of rare live butterflies and moths.

Arriving late, he rushed flustered into a spacious and humid hothouse packed with Jurassic-style foliage and dozens of unfettered fluttering wings. Spotting other media folk, he raced over asking "What's happening?" – hurriedly plonking his weighty camera case down with a thump, straight on top of one of the butterflies, squashing it and thereby making the species even rarer.

Happy snappers, not especially keen
to go on an assignment

In 1980 I joined a Press corps junket on the inaugural flight of the Royal Mail Air Service from Exeter to Liverpool to publicise this new way of speeding up the delivery of West Country letters and parcels. By 11pm the mail had been loaded aboard a smart new jet while the reporters – including local TV celebrities David Rogers and Judi Spiers from the then Westward Television station in Plymouth – had been stuffed into an old four-prop Dart Herald (not the smart new jet) which had definitely seen better days. As I sat in my seat waiting for the off, everything vibrating gently as the engines purred in readiness, I noticed the hands of the middle-aged photographer in the seat next to me gripping the arm rests with white-knuckled intensity.

"I haven't flown before," he said. The engine noise became louder and the plane began to move. "I don't like this," he said, his grip tightening.

We began accelerating rapidly. The fuselage was now shaking like a malaria victim and my colleague was looking like one, but we weren't lifting off; he even glanced out of the window next to him to ensure that the wing was still attached. The plane was taking so long to leave the ground that I was beginning to wonder if the runway was going to be long enough.

"I'm getting out," the photographer said, and tried to get up. "You can't," I said. "We're nearly..."

With a lurch that suggested not so much good piloting but that we had just vaulted a large unforeseen hedge, we were finally airborne and the land disappeared below in a cloud haze. The photographer calmed down, though he did look pale, and the instant we hit an air pocket he began talking about parachutes.

When we landed we spent an hour or so at Speke Airport taking a good look at the operation and had a less fraught journey home, arriving back at Exeter just before dawn.

"How was it?" I asked the photographer. "Piece of cake," he replied, but still didn't look like he could eat one.

The Printer

Here's a brief word about printers (from the days when we still had them in abundance).

Printers have a really dry wit. This was summed up for me by an exchange that took place with a Falmouth Packet linotype operator back in the 1970s. A linotype or "line-casting" machine, now largely redundant in the newspaper industry, has a typewriter keyboard; the operator taps in editorial and advertising copy and out pops a metal tablet with a line of type raised on the leading edge and a bunch of these are later hand-slotted into columns in a steel frame as part of creating a page.

The Linotype is fed by an open pot of molten lead on one side. One morning I was peering distractedly into this rather forbidding-looking container, waiting to ask the busy machinist about a change in some news text, when he looked up with a grave expression.

"You never want to put sugar in there, you know," he said.

I took a cautious step backwards and asked: "What, you mean it might explode?"

"No," was the deadpan reply. "No-one would drink it."

Linotype typesetter from 1958 (hdimagegallery).
Why does the operator look like comedian Jimmy Carr?

And this.

After a rather fractious day, a print manager unwisely pinned this printed sign to the works notice board.

Look after your boss – the next one could be worse.

The next morning, the following response had been added in biro:

Look after your men – the next boss might not have any!

The Result

So, this large assemblage of people all come together to produce your daily or weekly breakfast, evening or weekend read. The reporter has written his story, the sub-editor has either mangled it into some vague approximation of what you actually wrote or been very kind to those golden words; the photographer has taken his picture and the completed piece has been placed on a chosen page and that page and all the rest of the pages, each filled with other stories, pictures and advertisements, have gone off to the printers – and in no time the paper is on the newsstands. And, with a bit of luck, everything will be spelled correctly and the right way up.

Also – whilst not forgetting the dramatic "scoops" and the gritty revelations – it makes it all worthwhile to be able to come up with little tales like these.

A prisoner has given himself up after overstaying his home leave by 13 years. He turned up at the gates of Channings Wood Prison on Tuesday and asked: "Can I finish my sentence?" Shocked staff allowed him in and found he had failed to return from home leave in 1983, when still having eight months of a three-year sentence to complete.

A woman who appeared before magistrates on charges of stealing clothes from washing lines at night told police on arrest: "I am Dracula's daughter and I have to be home at dawn."

A swarm of bees took refuge under the asbestos roof of a lighting shed next to the projection booth of a Cornish cinema. The projection room door and windows had to be closed to keep the bees out and, as it was high summer, staff were "baking" inside the small cubicle. Every time a door banged, out came the bees. Eventually a bee expert doped the swarm and took them off to an apiary. The film showing at the time was "The Sting."

The only information shown yesterday on the electronic screen at Newton Abbot's railway station when a colleague caught his train was: *Notice to passengers. You wouldn't believe how long it takes to fix a simple fault like this.*

Bomb disposal experts blew up a "suspicious package" delivered to the

Exeter office of Devon's Euro MP Lord O'Hagan – only to find it contained Tory party leaflets.

When the Queen visited Newton Abbot as part of her Jubilee tour of Devon on August 5, 1977, her car whisked her through the throng so quickly that she was dubbed "the high-speed Queen." The party was behind schedule after leaving the Royal Yacht Britannia at Torquay and the driver's accelerator foot ensured the regal car took the appropriately-named Queen Street at a fair lick. Local dignitaries waiting on a platform outside Lloyds Bank nearly got whiplash trying to get a view of their speedy Monarch as her car nipped around Millets corner heading towards the racecourse. And the Queen barely gave the neglected civic party on their raised dais a glance, being more interested in the children on the other side of the road waving their little Union Jack pennants. It can be tough wearing a municipal chain (*also see part five*).

Part Two
Tools for the Job

Tools for the job
The delights of typewriters
Supplies supplies

Tools for the job

As anyone who has ever worked in an office of any kind will know, the one thing you need to make your day go effectively is the tools for the job: that is, things like a desk to sit at and fill up with your papers, sandwiches and Gonks, a chair to sit on, stationery to scribe on and a typewriter – or, nowadays, a computer or at least a serviceable chalkboard and abacus – to do the scribing.

Lose any of these precious items, or discover that they don't work properly, and you will find a measurable build up of stress accompanied by the odd feverish stare – especially when your superiors, who have little use for or knowledge of the tools of your trade, stare at you uncomprehendingly when you express your need for them.

I once completed a 900-word story and was poised to press SAVE (yes, I know I should have saved it as I was going, but the machine was in its infant stage, and so was I) when my company-acquired "back of a lorry" computer suddenly went dead, dispersing all my just-inputted data into the ether.

I went ballistic and stormed into the editor's office breathing vengeful words about our brand new but already-ailing system only to find the managing director sitting mildly in the chair opposite. He weathered the brief but energetic squall and, when the winds dropped, mildly responded to my query "What are we going to do about this?" with the calm and dismissive "Well, I don't know how these things work, anyway."

Here are a bunch of incidents regarding tools for the job that may ring a bell or two with the great deskbound majority.

The Delights of Typewriters

Going for a Czech-up

The heart of any reporter's world used to be his typewriter, now long replaced by the laptop or desktop computer (and the subsequent tablets, phones and satellite connections). There is something about the feel of a manual typewriter – a sense of excitement as you strike the keys and feel them give to the touch and bounce back again ready for more urgent prose. It's a feeling that is lost with the flat, plastic dullness of modem computer keyboards, efficient though they may be. But even an "old faithful" device has its time.

The typewriters used by one of my former news rooms had long passed their sell-by date. It was clear they were approaching museum status when someone mentioned they thought they had seen one of our machines in a Humphrey Bogart movie. And there were small engineering hiccoughs like carriages jamming, ribbons sticking and keys dropping off.

Anyway, one morning a company director arrived unheralded with three replacement machines in cardboard boxes. There was much excitement from director and editor as they revealed their prize, each imparting the glint-eyed enthusiasm of six-year-olds with a Christmas stocking.

Out came three cheap-looking portables with plastic shells and exceptionally thin metal attachments; a label revealed they were made in Czechoslovakia. Director and editor then spent some time poring over the typewriter manuals – which were unaccountably printed in German – before giving up and leaving the reporters to it.

One trainee reporter took her new machine, lifted the carriage return arm to release the carriage lock, wound a sheet of paper on to the roller, pressed the shift key... and a spring fell off, rendering the shift useless. The office typewriter mechanics were called.

Three days later, two cheery mechanics arrive, take one look at the machines and one asks: "Are they new?"

"Yes," says the editor, proudly.

"I thought they were," the mechanic replies. "I've never come across that make before. Where am I going to get parts for them?"

A weary sub looks up from his work, says "Czechoslovakia" and looks down again. The editor shoots him the kind of glance that would freeze custard.

Now the editor is forced to find out where the company obtained the new equipment and starts making a string of hurried phone calls. Eventually he gets the name of the English supplier.

"Ah," says mechanic one. "We know them. Send it back. If it's new they'll replace it."

The typewriters were never sent back or replaced, though the editor continued to undertake sporadic repairs. Eventually they were relegated to the top of a filing cabinet.

One day before that final resting place the editor decided to tackle the trainee's constantly rebellious Czech machine, which had more problems than a bricked-up, wheel-less Lada. He spent ages reattaching a tiny, insubstantial little spring and then presented the mended article to the trainee with a mixture of triumph and relief.

She lifted the carriage return arm to release the carriage lock, wound a sheet of paper on to the roller, pressed the shift key... and the spring fell off again.

"You did that on purpose!" he said.

A while later...

Trainee
This crummy typewriter is playing up again.
Editor
You know it was serviced while you were on holiday.
Trainee
Yes, I know it had a new spring...

Stool Bitchin

One day, in a spectacular and no doubt genuinely benevolent cost-cutting exercise, an editor I knew arrived with a carload of typing stools which he appeared to have rummaged from a skip. All of them looked like they had been used as dodgem cars, with their backs twisted, their upholstery torn or ragged, and their feet failing to meet the floor at the same time, giving them a seasick rocking motion. The staff took one look and instantly made the right decision by walking away as swiftly as possible.

Undeterred, the editor set about refurbishing the contorted, uncomfortable and unstable stools using cloth, foam, scissors, sticky-back plastic and a staple gun. But there were still no takers and the stools remained clustered at one end of the office like a gaggle of disabled geese until they were dumped in the gents' lavatory, alongside piles of back copies of the paper.

This may have put them out of sight, out of mind for an editor whose passion for early seventies office furniture renovation had obviously run its course, but getting to the urinals became a serious obstacle course and the stools eventually returned whence they had come, to another skip, looking slightly better dressed but unaccountably smelling of wee and disinfectant urinal pucks.

As mentioned in the above, some bright spark decided to store back issues of the newspaper in the Gents toilet. The old editions were moved in and stacked in neat piles because there was allegedly no room for them anywhere else in the building.

One morning, one of the reporters was standing at the porcelain apparatus, whistling happily and idly dowsing a blue antiseptic urinal cake in the momentary calm, when the door opened and in walked one of the advertising girls.

"Oh," she said, hardly batting an eyelid, "I knocked three times and there was no reply" and she began rifling through the nearest pile of yellowing newsprint. She eventually found the issue she was looking for and hurried off leaving the interrupted reporter looking flushed and hiding his own pink attachments behind the company's ivory plumbing.

Keyboard brutality

Surprisingly, or perhaps not, most reporters are not touch typists. It is quite sufficient for most of them to bash away meaningfully on a keyboard with two fingers. An exceptionally gifted journo typist bashes away with two fingers on each hand! One colleague who acquired a computer after years of using a typewriter continued to hit the light plastic keys with the same severity he had shown his old steel monster and within months had stripped away most of the lettering.

Editor
(*fiddling about with his troublesome typewriter*)
Now what's gone wrong with the blasted thing?

Self
(*from a safe distance*)
It needs throwing across the room.

Editor
I bow to someone with experience.
[Result: Me 1, Editor 1]

By the way, at this point I want to publicly emphasize that there is NO TRUTH in a spurious story that I once "threw a typewriter across the office."

(Not true)

I deny it fervently and always have. Nevertheless the tale lingers on like a party drunk, repeated as recently as 2013, sixteen years after my early retirement. Not once in my long career has this happened. Cub's honour (I didn't make it to the Scouts). However, that does not mean I have never caused injury to a typewriter. Sadly, I have – though mainly unintentionally.

The first time was when I worked in a public library and I had to use the library's old black Imperial typewriter (the sort you usually see in forties films about news rooms); my job was to create library file cards, book tags and to cut stencils of stock lists, and so on. It was coming to the end of its days – and they had been long days even for something so sturdily built – and it was me who drew the short straw and retired it from use.

One day I was tapping away at some library cards when one of the striking arms suddenly snapped. Sheared off clean as a whistle and rattled away into the interior. As irony would have it, it was the letter L, which meant that my colleagues could rightly say I'd "knocked the L out of it."

Much later, when I was working from a district news office I became the proud user of a massive, lime green Hermes Ambassador, a typewriter which appeared to have been built for the tank corps. It was huge, heavy and almost impossible to lift without hearing a ping in an area of your physique from which you least want to hear such a sound. It also had big rubber feet, which meant it was anchored to the desk top and could not be easily pushed across the work surface to make room for other things.

"You'll want a mat for that," my Editor said helpfully. "I'll get one."

He produced a large maroon floor tile, which was presumably one left over from his popular DIY enterprises. I heaved the machine on to it but it still wouldn't slide over the desk top. So I removed the tile and flipped it over, so that the rubber side was under the Hermes and the fabric side was on the desk. Now it worked fine. The flexibility of the fabric under the weight of the machine allowed just enough movement for me to slide the thing out of the way. Brilliant, I thought, and went home.

Overnight the office cleaner took it into her head to vigorously polish all the desks. I came in the next morning, sat down and pushed the Hermes back to make space for my notebook. Now floating on a silky surface of silicone, the typewriter and its mat flew away from me like an overweight ice dancer, disappeared off the end of the desk, hit the floor with a mighty crash and its carriage cracked. The floor actually bowed briefly with the weight and the receptionist in the outer office nearly had a grand mal.

"No-one's ever broken one of these before," a mechanic told me.

I blamed the floor tile.

On the only other occasion of physical typewriter abuse that I can recall I hit the Hermes' smaller cousin so hard, in a fit of stress-related pique, that its carriage jammed and we had to call in the mechanic once more. Kindly, no-one said a word. I think they were keeping their heads down, fearful that I might (as per legend) throw a (lighter) typewriter across the office...

Part of a vintage trade advert for an Underwood typewriter, with added speech bubble

Anyone Remember the Supplies Joke?
"Supplies, supplies..."

Being in an office is rather like being in prison, with the thankful exception that at least you get to go home at night, or at some time in the calendar when your boss permits it. You find yourself locked up with the same people, sometimes gazing out through a nearby window at the exterior world and wishing you were anywhere but here (rather like me at secondary school during maths lessons). And whilst you try to get on with the other inmates, who are all afflicted with the same malady (though there's always one who would like to be there 24/7), there is no guarantee that your day-to-day will be harmonious. Especially when you want the tools of the trade...

Stationary Stationery

Beeno wanted to get some stationery from the stationery cupboard and went down the corridor to speak to receptionist Harriet Lang, who had been in charge of dispensing items like pens, pencils, envelopes and so on since the Dawn of Mankind. You would ask her for whatever you wanted and she would go to the stationery cupboard, unlock it, and bring the said item to you when she had a moment. On this day, however, things were to be different. Or not.

Harriett said: "I've got nothing to do with stationery any more. You'll have to ring David at the accounts offices."

The accounts offices were located in a separate building about half a mile away, so Beeno walked back to his office and rang David. David's colleague Mary answered.

Mary: "Oh, David's nothing to do with stationery anymore."

Beeno: "Well, who is?"

Mary didn't know so Beeno asked to speak to her boss. He was on the phone. So he spoke to David, who appeared to have reappeared.

David: "Harriett's in charge of stationery."

Beeno: "She's just told me you were."

David says no and to ring Harriett's boss, advertising manager Clarence Mildly.

Increasingly annoyed as he "only wanted a bloody pencil," Beeno walks back down the corridor and into Clarence's office. He relates the sad tale to a barely interested Clarence, enrobed in his customary cloak of cheap cigar smoke.

Finally Beeno hears the reply: "Harriet's in charge. It's just that I haven't told her yet."

Oh, how the scream of frustration could be heard as far away as Stockholm.

Anyway, Beeno returns to Harriett and again requests access to the stationery cupboard. Harriet says she's too busy to deal with it now and will deal with it later.

"But I only want a *pencil*," Beeno entreats.

"Oh, all right," grumps Harriet. Then, after walking down the corridor and opening the dark green steel doors of the company treasure trove announces: "We've run out. I'll order some."

Beeno, before stomping off to buy one at Smiths, asks for B pencils.

"I don't know about that."

"Well, can you just get a single box of Bs for me. That's what I use, and as I'm the only one in the office with decent shorthand I'd like the right pencils," he adds, a tad conceitedly.

The pencils arrive some days later. There are two boxes of 12 and they are all HB.

Editor to Beeno: "Oh, just buy your own box and put it on your expenses." Which he does.

Bumf!

Harriet had to borrow some toilet paper from the Gents as there was none in the Ladies loo. She asked one of the reporters to collect a roll and then carefully unravelled the required amount before handing it back. Afterwards she returned to Editorial to thank them for the life-saving deed.

Immediately trainee Whitney cried out: "We want it back!"

Joining in the joke, Beeno added: "Yes. We recycle our toilet paper."

"Edwin recently brought in one of his own toilet rolls from home when we were short, "Adrian chimed in. "It says a lot for this newspaper when the Editor has to bring in one of his own toilet rolls."

The same problem arose a few days later and this time Harriet decided to approach the Editor. He seemed concerned that she knew he had a toilet roll in one of his desk drawers, as if it was stuffed with secret personnel files or guidelines on how to open the stationery cupboard with a paper clip.

He took the roll out cautiously and then, anxious not to let it out of his grasp, asked the astounded receptionist: "How many sheets do you want?"

In fact, he did "loan" her the precious toilet roll rather than counting out each leaf. But later, when Edwin was out, Harriet came back to complain.

"It's ridiculous," she said indignantly. "Asking how many sheets I was going to use!"

"Well, it's not an unreasonable request," replied Beeno with a satirical grin. "It's down to volume. I mean, each sheet has got two sides, you know."

At which Harriet walked off spluttering.

Apparently some toilet rolls must have been ordered from the Accounts and Office Stationary Monitoring Department as, after a two-day wait, FOUR toilet rolls arrived accompanied by the (hopefully facetious) handwritten note *These have got to last a month.*

String

We all like to hang on to what is "ours" in a busy office – pens (which walk), paper clips (which unaccountably disappear from tidy trays), staplers (that rarely end up in a jelly, as in *The Office*, but still find their way effortlessly into someone else's drawer with the owner's sticky name tag still attached), toilet rolls, even string.

Receptionist Harriet Lang enters the news room and looks around at the three occupants.

Harriet: Has anyone got any string?

There is a general silence except for some typing sounds, which continue. Clearly the request, if heard, is considered so low a priority that it fails to register.

Harriet (*batting on regardless*): Or the keys to the editor's office. The string's in there.

Sub-editor Sam: I haven't got any string, and Edwin's office is locked. He's out.

Harriet: Who's got the key?

Sam: Edwin.

Harriet (*disbelievingly*): Come on...

Sam: He's taken his keys with him.

Chief reporter Beeno (*remembering his absent sub-editor. Unhelpfully*): Tom's got a set of keys. But he's on holiday in Canada.

Harriet: What, and taken them with him?

Sam: They're probably at home.

Harriet: Oh, hell.

Sam: Sorry.

Harriet: This is ridiculous.

Beeno: True.

Harriet: What's he got in there, the Crown Jewels?

Reporter Teebone (*quiet until now, impatiently, without looking up from his typewriter*): He's got string...

Nothing, Nothing (at all)

Harriet wanders into the news room and hovers about expectantly.

Beeno: What do you want?

Harriet: Nothing.

Beeno: I think we've got some of that. I'll go and look. If I haven't got any I won't bring it to you.

Harriet: That's fair enough.

Soap Opera

I

Harriet went to the Ladies to find there was no soap, so she went to the accounts department, where all the company's office supplies were kept, to get some. When she asked for a bar she was told to (a) get some soap from the Gents, or (b) use hot water only.

When she insisted, she was told "Oh, Mary has the keys to the cupboard where the soap is kept and she's left them at home."

II

Teebone: "The company chairman must have been down yesterday, there's a bar of soap in the loo."

Beeno: "Is it *that* time of the year again?"

Deputy editor (*scowl*).

III

Cheery note for retiring Union officer and Father of the Chapel

LOOK ON THE BRIGHT SIDE...

... AT LEAST THERE WAS HALF A BAR OF SOAP IN THE GENTS WHEN YOU LEFT!

Disappearing Envelopes

Adrian: I put some envelopes on top of the filing cabinets last week and they've all gone.

Sam: Where did you put them?

Adrian: Up here (*points*).

Sam: Well, they've been crying out for envelopes for weeks in the district office – and you put those envelopes in the district office box, for collection by the courier, so no wonder they've gone.

Adrian (*picking up box which has FOR DISTRICT OFFICE written on it*): Is that for them? Oh, I just thought it was an old box. I never take any notice of it.

Sam and Beeno: Sigh...

Brush Off

Editor Edwin spots a ratty old nail brush in Photographic and realises that it's his, normally resident on the side of a basin in the Gents' toilet. An inquest then ensues on what the plastic wedge with its nylon bristles is doing in the photo lab.

"That's my nail brush," says Edwin, without room for contradiction. "I brought it here fifteen years ago!"

The two photographers are unable to solve the great mystery of its relocation and Edwin leaves with his prized antique after one of them grudgingly ventures: "Perhaps it was one of the cleaners."

Beeno, aware of the ineffectiveness of the rarely-appearing domestics, adds: "If it's our cleaners they certainly wouldn't be using it to clean anything."

Copy This!

As I mention elsewhere, in the days before computers, when we were all bashing away on typewriters, we wrote our stories on what was known as "copy paper" and took carbon copies of our glowing prose in case the originals were lost (and they often were).

Now these fragile pieces of copy paper were newsprint off cuts, specially chopped to size for reporters' use. At the time, newsprint was the cheapest paper you could find. OK, companies had to buy it in huge, expensive rolls, but if you went to a stationers to buy some (assuming they would stock it, which they wouldn't) they would probably say something like "Here, take it, we've got loads of the stuff. None of our customers want it and its blocking up the stairwell."

Anyway, on with the story, told to me in some detail after the event.

The editor of one of the company's string of local weeklies was at the central print works, where all the titles in the group were printed. He had almost run out of copy paper in his district office so decided to set about getting some more from the case room. He asked the chap in charge and he was about to guillotine a pile to size when one of the company directors appeared and demanded to know what was going on. The chap in charge told him. The director turned to the editor.

"You can't have any."

A flabbergasted editor replied: "Why?"

"Because your lot haven't paid their bills for it [*copy paper*] for the last six weeks."

"That's not my responsibility!"

In desperation, the editor rang the managing director who referred him to the group editor, the one in overall editorial charge of all the titles.

His response: "Oh, have a look around in some of the cupboards down there and see if you can find some."

"Are you suggesting I *steal* some?"

"No, no. Just have a look around."

Replying that he was too busy to conduct a clandestine rummage, the frustrated editor left it at that, though he still had none of the apparently gold-standard copy paper to take back to his desk.

In the end the editor in chief sent over a batch of copy paper from his own newsroom to help re-stock his colleague's branch office. Presumably the constraining bill was then paid and matters calmed down.

Before that, one of the reporters watching the relief copy paper vanish from his own office commented: "What happens when OUR copy paper runs out? Will it be down to W.H. Smith's for some A4?"

Footnote:

That's the typing paper A4, not the route from London to Bristol, which I am certain was not being chopped into manageable chunks for retail sale, though anything is possible during times of austerity.

Complete Mug

Beeno drops his prized *WISPA* mug on the floor – the one he got free in a chocolate bar promotion; he would never actually *buy* one – and it cracks. He throws it away, despite sub Tom's suggestion that it be donated to the local museum. Suddenly the editor, who has overheard this exchange, calls

Beeno into his office. He is holding a pale, white mug promoting a local radio station. It is packed with all sorts of writing instruments.

"I'm tired of looking at this," he says. And who wouldn't be? It was pretty uninspiring. "Would you like it?"

Beeno accepts the unexpected gesture with a "Thank you."

Edwin: "I'll wash it out."

Beeno (*hastily*): "That's all right, I'll do it."

Edwin: "I insist."

He takes a wodge of copy paper from Beeno's desk and, under the disbelieving gaze of the mug-less one, who has that sinking feeling coming on, Edwin exits to the Gents. He returns moments later with the "cleaned" mug and hands it to Beeno.

Edwin: "That'll put lead in your pencil."

He exits chuckling and Beeno examines the gift cautiously, like someone setting a mousetrap and anxious not to trip the spring-loaded bar across his thumb. Words like salmonella drift across his mind. He writes to a friend: *Why is it every cup of tea now tastes of chinagraph pencil? Urk! Head hits desk. Call the vet...*

Clipped

A reporter once took the long trek up to the company's aforementioned Accounts and Office Stationary Monitoring Department to get some paper clips as the news room was getting seriously low. These innocuous little metal fasteners were important to editorial at the time, as they were used to keep important documents together.

For instance, every reporter would clip together all the pages of each of his stories and also attach any pertinent photograph or artwork; this small package, and many others like it, would go to the sub-editor who would reclip each piece after his input and then put all the stories for a particular page (a real-size sheet laid out in pencil to show text, pictures and advertisement spaces) into that page, fold it all up and clip it together. *With paper clips*. These bundles would then be taken to the main print works for processing. So the paper clips were vital, and to run out would create all sorts of problems.

Anyway, this long-winded introduction leads to this silly denouement.

Beeno, for it was he, arrived to collect his stash of paper clips from the Keepers of the Holy Stationary, having telephoned beforehand to check they had some in stock. Expecting a box of at least 500, due to their continual use and the fact that the printers rarely returned them to source, he was surprised when one of the Guardians of Office Supplies produced a large brown envelope.

"Hold out your hands," he said.

Beeno cupped his palms whilst raining an anticipatory eyebrow.

The Guardian gradually poured out about twenty paper clips.

"What's this?" Beeno asked.

"The paper clips you asked for."

"I want at least a box."

"Well, this is all we've got," was the reply, as the Guardian generously inched out another dozen or so.

"Well, you'd better order some," Beeno advised.

He put the meagre offerings in a pocket and walked back to the newsroom to ask his editor if he would deal with office supplies from now on.

Part 3

About Me

About me
Here we go

About me

In order to provide a bit of background for all this: I was born in Falmouth, Cornwall, into a Victorian-principled matriarchal family living in a large terraced house that comprised myself, my parents, an uncle, grandmother, a sheepdog and a cluster of ostentatious aunts, all now deceased.

My family had no history of journalism or anything like it, having seafaring connections instead, on the masculine side. But my father George was skilled at art and used to write stories to read to me when I was little. It was my own passion for books, writing and drawing that attracted me to newspapers.

But it was not the investigative reporting of "Watergate" bloodhounds Woodward and Bernstein or the vivid radio reports about America from the late, great Alistair Cooke that drew me towards a news desk (although they helped). It was another journalistic icon altogether. It was Tintin.

I had started reading the Tintin adventures, created by Belgian artist Herge (Georges Prosper Remi), from primary school age, and his redoubtable Belgian reporter, who had many exotic escapades but never seemed to do much actual reporting, probably became a kind of fictional mentor in my chosen profession. Herge's skilled draughtsmanship and his exciting and comic tales of intrigue in exotic, far-off locations with unconventional characters had a lingering impact on me, because when I moved to a secondary school I began drawing cartoon stories about my classroom pals, filling more than two dozen red Silvine notebooks with a bunch of these unsophisticated adventures between 1959 and 1963. Me and my friends (my friends and I?) got involved in motor racing, fighting old Nazi villains and even battling a race of dangerous tentacled aliens. Unsurprisingly, several of the later stories revolved around a fictional newspaper.

Here's how the teenage me pictured myself in the early 1960s as a future newshound in a story called *The Case of the Unwanted Invention*. I didn't smoke then; it just seemed part of a reporter's genetic makeup to have him – me – puffing away on the other side of the ribbon.

I began my working life as a library assistant, where I came across such joyous human eccentricities as the borrower who used a slice of cooked bacon as a bookmark and the borough engineer who felt that the best (read *cheapest*) way to improve the lighting in the lending library was to simply lower the strip light clusters – and as these were slung directly over the 10ft high bookcases, the result was brilliant illumination for the dusty top of each case and deeper shadows either side, where the books were.

Falmouth Public Library filled five years of my life before I became an advertising assistant with the *Falmouth Packet* newspaper. After a couple of years I left to spend a short while working as a school photographer in Yorkshire before returning to the *Packet* for another, longer and more rewarding stint, latterly moving into its Editorial department.

When I finally transferred to the editorial side (thanks to the graciousness and good judgement of the then editor, the late Roy Standing), I realised it was exactly what I'd always wanted to do. But, ironically, after 18 months of diligent scribing I was made redundant. The company apparently needed to lose two editorial staff in a cost-cutting purge, using the established business maxim of "last in, first out."

Fortunately, within days I was offered a job at the *Mid-Devon Advertiser* as, at that time, both papers were in the same ownership. The MDA editor Lance Samson and I already knew each other from Packet days and I got an interview immediately.

How I recorded my booting-out in my diary of February 6, 1975

I drove up to Devon on a grey Sunday in March, armed only with the paper's address and a rudimentary map of how to get there. When I arrived at Newton Abbot – then noted as a premier market town and railway centre – I stopped and asked directions to the newspaper offices. "Never heard of it, mate," was the inspiring reply. And that was my introduction to my new home.

I did eventually find the MDA offices, at that time resident in an old wooden shack, a former Territorial Army centre hidden from the main thoroughfare on a small industrial slip road by a tyre fitting garage and a lofty bank of used tyres. I passed the interview, which was pretty much a formality, and started work there – appropriately enough, as these ramblings indicate – on Fool's Day, April 1.

Two weeks after my unceremonious exit from the *Packet*, I was offered my old job back. Obviously the managers in the nice offices with the river view (as opposed to the newsroom view of a stone wall) had had a rethink. I declined the belated offer and stayed in Devon.

During my newspaper career I generally found local communities to be packed with kind, generous, witty and receptive people and enjoyed reporting all sorts of issues over more than two decades.

But the job can be tough – both from the long hours and the relentless internal "politics" – and I finally took early retirement in 1997, stressed and exhausted, accepting my new challenge in much the same way as a British POW brightens when he finds a half-dug and undiscovered escape tunnel under his bunk.

Even so, I remember one exchange at the time with a similarly-retreating colleague.

Me: "Bet you're glad to be retiring."

Him: "Too right. I've had enough of it all."

Me: "How many years is it now?"

Him: "Too many. I'm thankful it's finally over."

Me: "I see you're coming back part-time on Tuesday..."

As for me, I'd really had enough.

The snapshots in this book took place in both Devon and Cornwall at a number of locations on several weekly and evening titles involving a vast canvas of amazing personalities. It is in part a biography, as the inclusion of its author is unavoidable and helps set the scene. But mainly it aims to reflect that time-honoured journalistic position of sitting at the back, listening to other people's vocalisations, taking notes and then recording the result in text for others to enjoy – and to give them a good chuckle or two at the expense of me, my colleagues and some of the "clients" I met along the way.

It was a privilege to be part of it all and I made some wonderful friends and gracious "contacts," though it was not always quite the amazing Tintinesque fantasy scenario I had anticipated.

Or, on rethinking that comment, perhaps it was...

Here We Go...

I remember once – very early in my career – being assigned to find the owner of an out-of-the-way caravan site who had apparently been harassing his tenants in an attempt, as far as I remember, to get them to abandon the place so that he could sell the land for housing. The site was on the far outskirts of a small Cornish village and its owner lived in an adjoining house. When I got to the village I pulled over and asked directions.

"Down there 'bout two mile and take the first left after the barn," I was told – or something like that. So I followed the instructions to the letter – which is probably not a good idea in Cornwall where the actual location of places and even the number of miles needed to be travelled in order to get to them have always been a mite ambiguous. Still, I got to the barn OK, saw a nearby turning and pulled over into an unexpectedly wide lay-by.

There was a tractor-width entrance in the high hedge and a descending woodland lane. This was a bit too narrow for the car, so I got out and I began walking. Unfortunately, the lane quickly became a rutted path, then grew narrower – and muddier – as it meandered to the right through the trees and levelled out. By the time it had meandered to the left again the ground was flat and waterlogged.

The water was half-way up my shoes and, as I was dressed in a suit and black office brogues - no boots - I was beginning to have second thoughts. Then I saw the building. It looked like a regular cottage at first, with a flat roof. As I got closer – notebook in one hand, stepping cautiously on some floating planks in a vain attempt to keep my socks and trouser turn-ups dry from the chocolaty water and optimistically calling the name of the man I wanted to interview – I realised I was approaching a disused pig house.

I squelched back to the main road, largely on tip-toe, got in the car, drove off and – twenty yards later, around a sharp right-hand bend, I came across the caravan site – with the owner's home conspicuously next door. The objectors were at home but their landlord was not. I returned to the office where I finished the story by telephone and waited for the mud to dry.

It was the first of many ignominious moments.

Bus-ted

Like the time I reported a rather startling incident where a double-decker bus left the road on a residential estate, slid down a 20ft slope and ploughed into a council house, making a huge hole in the first floor bedroom wall. A sleeping 23-year-old found her feet buried in glass and rubble and was only saved from serious head injuries because she had turned her bed around 90 degrees a week earlier on a whim. No-one else was hurt.

I covered this tale, visiting the site with a photographer and interviewing all those involved, but badly turned my ankle in a pot hole. I limped back to the office, wrote the story in quite a bit of pain and then got a lift home to recuperate as my ankle had swelled up like a football. I was comforted by being told that my story was going to appear on the front page on Friday. Which would mean I would get my first page one by-line – that's your name on your story, in a little box – which was a big thing for me then, in my fledgling years; a star entry for my cuttings album.

Come publication day, the colourful balloon of fame had popped as the story appeared with the by-line "By Staff Reporters." I asked why. The chief reporter told me: "You were off sick so another reporter had to finish it." This other reporter had added just *one paragraph* on the end of the tale about the later removal of the bus by crane. I was devastated, knowing it could be many months before I had another stab at a front page lead, being near the bottom of the pecking order.

Still, I could always smile at the photograph showing the green double decker wedged in the wall carrying an advertising strip reading: RELAX BY BUS.

In fact, buses were my first job as a reporter with the *Packet* – my first real reporting assignment anywhere, actually. The chief reporter gave me a cutting from the *Western Morning News* about an upcoming Western National bus strike and said: "Get me something on that – how it's going to affect services in our circulation area."

So, off I went ringing bus company chiefs and union officials, using the names and numbers scribbled under BUSES in the office Contacts Book. Then I wrote it all up on my trusty red, plastic-shelled portable typewriter on sheets of off-white and aforementioned "copy paper" – i.e. gash bits of newsprint, cut to roughly a demy quarto size at 11.5in x 7in and about the lowest form of paper, slightly above a cheap lavatory roll in quality – ready for its long journey.

This would take it to the sub-editor (who edited the piece and found a spot for it on a page of the next edition of the popular broadsheet), to the linotype operator (who set my glowing words in even more glowing hot metal), to the page-setter, the reader (who checked it for errors on a galley-proof) and finally into print, among a host of other stories and pictures, locked into a metal frame and hoisted with other identical frames the size of our newspaper page into the body of a colossal printing machine fed by giant rolls of newsprint some 54in wide and about as thick.

One on the bonce...

I took part in a charity go-kart event at Newton Abbot Racecourse in 1982 and was one of the amateur drivers who had an appropriately-named "Crackpots' Hour" set aside for them.

During the practise lap all seemed to be going well until I became gripped by overconfidence, with inevitable consequences. Remember that these carts are pretty fast and very low to the asphalt and, as I lost control of my vehicle, I became overcome with a state that humorist Gerard Hoffnung described as "losing one's presence of mind." Instead of braking, I found my foot glued resolutely to the accelerator pedal, the track disappearing behind me and the barriers, the stands and the road outside looming uncomfortably close.

With my speed increasing, the kart went into a spin and I slewed off the track heading for a pile of tractor tyres, laid out for just the purpose of restraining reckless idiots like me from ploughing into the supportive crowd. I hit the pile with a thump and one of these huge tyres (which I'm assured weigh between 400 and 600 pounds – that's about as heavy as an oil drum or a young male lion) coiled into the air and clumped down on my head and shoulder.

Fortunately I was wearing a helmet and it was only a glancing blow; but it was the kind of glance that tells you in one look not to do such a daft thing again. I took note of the advice, left the race and never got into a go kart again, making the world (or at least the track) a safer place.

Just one for the road...

Hasty...

You have to be careful when you make what you consider is a firm, incontrovertible judgement at the time of writing a story. You may think something has been set in stone. But you quickly learn that history, and people, assure that nothing remains permanent, and there's always a playful sub around to remind you of this.

In April 1983 I wrote a story which began: *Kingsteignton Council reverted to parish status on Wednesday night with the historic words 'Hooray, we are now a village, chaps.'*

However, the ancient Devon settlement, which had been a village for centuries and was often dubbed the largest such community in the country, had only the previous year decided to adopt town council status.

So when I submitted the new piece saying they had changed their minds, the subs desk could not resist the following, quoting my previous dramatic story from only eight months before.

"Since July 21, 1982, Kingsteignton has been a town. It is no longer the second largest village in England. It will never be a village again."

The immortal words of Brian 'finger on the pulse' Thomas. August 6, 1982.

Ironically, the parish council re-adopted town status in 2009 and the former village still remains a town at the time of writing this paragraph.

Unless, yet again, I have tempted providence...

Part Four
Not a Packet of Tea

Introduction to a newspaper
Park ye not on ye grass
Other Packet snippets

Introduction to a Newspaper

When I first arrived at the *Falmouth Packet* in 1969 its headquarters was housed in an oddly-shaped, cream-coloured building on the southern bank of a tributary of the River Fal between Falmouth and its smaller neighbour Penryn.

It was part of a riverside ribbon of boat builders' yards and light industrial premises and the waters alongside were always packed with anchored pleasure craft and small cargo vessels heading upstream to off-load coal and timber at Penryn Quay. At low tide the navigable channel reduced to a thin, shallow snake and the familiar scent of the extensive surrounding mud flats tended to pervade everything.

The advertising office was on the first floor of the two-storey building and when it rained we had to put out jugs and buckets to catch the drips from the ceiling thanks to the insecure roof.

I'd not been there very long when plans to knock the place down and rebuild were announced. But, in an attempt to "keep the presses rolling," the owners decided to allow rebuilding work to take place while the offices were still occupied.

NO - THE WORKMAN HAVEN'T QUITE FINISHED THE OFFICE.......

So the grounds were caked in mud, mechanical diggers began racing around like stock cars and the sporadic grinding of pneumatic drills ensured many phone conversations were one-way.

Walls would disappear overnight to be replaced by tarpaulin, then by thin wooden skins, and a thin film of dust began settling over work surfaces, work and workers.

Having fun with your big drill...

...and your digger

...and your little drill

In order to make room for this organised chaos most of the staff cars were relocated to park along the grass verge outside – one of the busiest roads in the area – much to the annoyance of the police whose principal complaint was apparently not so much about road safety but that we were churning up the wide strip of grass between the pavement and the road.

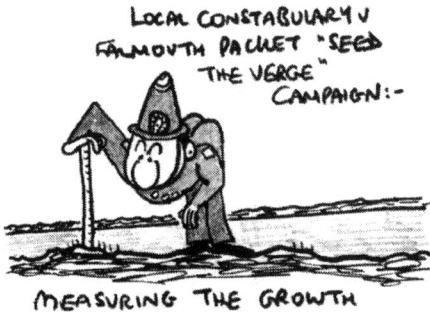

Still, the contractors got the job done in good time and the paper was delivered a block of spanking new offices. The advertising and editorial departments ended up on the road side looking out on a high wall, while the management and accounts offices ended up overlooking the picturesque river. Strange, that...

And, being so close to the river, we always wondered what would happen to our nice, new wooden building if there was a Biblical-style downpour. Would we end up floating away?

Anyway, we got a brand new press, a web offset plant, which changed the *Packet's* whole printing process from stone-assembled page frames to photographic plate production and where a continuous roll of paper is fed through the printing press. It was enormous, but it changed the face of the paper almost overnight.

Historical footnote:

Incidentally, the *Falmouth Packet* is named after the great Post Office Packet sailing ships that between 1688 and 1852 carried cargoes of bullion, mail, goods and passengers to and from Falmouth and Spain and West India. Right, that's enough history for the moment.

Park Ye Not on Ye Grass

As I said, while the Falmouth Packet was being rebuilt around us most of the staff cars, and there were quite a few, were relocated to parking along the grass verge outside.

The newspaper building (it's elsewhere now) was below the level of the main road – then the main route into town – and separated from the busy thoroughfare by a high stone wall, of modest height at road level, and then by a wide pavement and a similarly wide verge.

This relocation of vehicles caused considerable trepidation amongst the local police whose principal complaint, as I previously mentioned, was not so much about road safety infringements (as we were on a concave bend and could not be accused of blocking motorists' views of the way ahead) but that we were churning up the grass!

When it was eventually explained to the boys in blue that we had little alternative but to relocate our cars due to the extent of the works some sort of grudging compromise was reached with the understanding that we would "'Op off aht of it" once safe parking became available around the new office block.

I couldn't resist illustrating, and exaggerating, this rather silly spat at the time.

On one particularly miserable Tuesday
morning in February the idyllic calm
of the PACKET's charming mud-soaked
pastures was shattered by the arrival
of a little man in blue and

THE LOCAL CONSTABULARY v
FALMOUTH PACKET "CONSERVE
A VERGE" SCHEME

GENTLEMAN-IN-WAITING

① SEEDING THE SOIL

② FLATTENING THE BUMPS

③ MEASURING THE GROWTH

③ PROTECTING FROM THE HARMS OF TRAFFIC

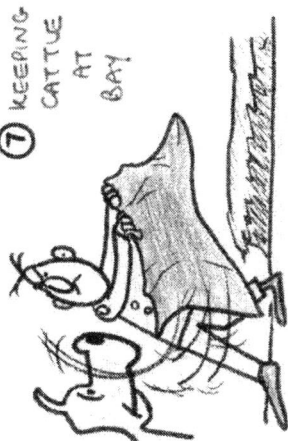

⑤ REMOVAL OF ROAD-SIDE PESTS

⑥ PROTECTING FROM THE WEATHER

④ TENDERLY TENDING THE SEEDS

⑦ KEEPING CATTLE AT BAY

UNFORTUNATELY

P.T.O.

(9) OVER ENTHUSIASM?

Other Packet Snippets
The Bedside Book

THE
Falmouth Packet
BEDSIDE BOOK

No 3½	FRIDAY OCTOBER 43, 1822	£2-10-0

NEARLY 5 COUNCIL TENANTS FACE A 1970 RENT INCREASE OF ¼d IN THE £1 !!!

B SID THUMB (MAMAC)

BIFF (!) GOES A POLICE CAR.

In 1970 I created a parody called *The Falmouth Packet Bedside Book* – the original now a mite faded and water-damaged – which featured imaginary matters of the day at the *Packet* and drawings of many of the staff. In 2013 I unearthed the antique booklet from a scruffy cardboard box stuffed with vintage exercise books, including the *Our Pals* series of adventures with my secondary school chums and my own *Mad* magazine styled series *Queer* (not a good title in modern PC days, but then intended to merely indicate the odd or curious) where I created parodies of TV shows of the day.

I loaned the bedside book to my long-standing journalist friend Mike Truscott, a former *Packet* staffer and latterly a biography ghost writer (though not in a sheet, rattling chains), handing it over when he came up to Newton Abbot from Falmouth for a lunch date. Afterwards he kindly emailed to say he had read every word of it on the train on the way back and confessed "I had forgotten just how genuinely funny (an exceedingly difficult genre, as I'm sure you know) your work is..."

Who needs to be nationally or internationally recognised when you receive such frank and fulsome responses as this from a professional colleague? I went on to illustrate one of Mike's books, *Reflections*, the following year which he compiled from some of his contemporary *Packet* freelance columns to raise funds for Cancer Research.

The parody headlines on the front of the bedside book, in the spirit of "local" papers, were:

NEARLY FIVE COUNCIL TENANTS FACE A 1970 RENT INCREASE OF A FARTHING IN THE POUND
by Sid Thumb (Maniac) (*the lead story*)
BIFF GOES A POLICE CAR (*hitting a bus*)
MR I.M.A. TWIT EATS A LAND ROVER
Visiting visitor from abroad "just passing through" (*and pictured from the back, ha ha*)
Visit from the Australian Prime Minister (*headline upside down, ho ho*)
and the totally unacceptable ABLE SEAMAN RAPES ELEPHANT (*a rather tasteless and unoriginal play on the naval fellow being "able." He he. Not really... Too many* Carry On *films, methinks.*)

Tea and Trago

My advertising manager came from London and had taken the post as a pre-retirement job. He was a lovely fellow, a bit too keen on the falling down sauce, but would always invite the department members to a Christmas party at his home. These were delightful, happy occasions and the high spot of each December: to quote him, "mighty fine."

Whenever he answered the office phone and someone north of the River Tamar queried "Falmouth *Packet*?" he would suck on his pipe languidly and clarify: "Yes, like a packet of tea, old boy."

At the time, in the late 1960s, an advertising rep would always drive up from Falmouth to Liskeard to collect that week's copy for the Trago Mills full page advert. Trago Mills, for those unfamiliar with the establishment (and there can't be too many of those), is a privately-run retail chain with branches in Liskeard, Newton Abbot and Falmouth. The Liskeard run was a 92 mile round trip and took a good three hours, including park-and-collect.

Sometimes the week's copy would be retrieved from the *Cornish Guardian* offices, which also ran the ads, as did (and do) a host of other West Country papers, and sometimes from the offices of the Liskeard branch of the store, from the very hands of Trago's robust founder the late Mike Robertson.

Mr Robertson was a forthright man who wrote his own weekly column within his advertisement, commenting on subjects commercial and political, under the pseudonym "Tripehound." He also liked to take a pot at local planners whenever they refused one of his development schemes and we would always have to collect the copy with enough time to spare before publication so that we could pass it through the hands of our legal advisors, who mostly let it pass unaltered.

On one occasion my boss decided to make the journey, both to meet Mr Robertson and to enjoy a relaxing summer drive on picturesque Cornish A and B roads. Unfortunately, he got lost and took ages coming back. We thought he'd indulged a few ales and ended up in a ditch, but fortunately all was well and he returned before the witching hour (when legal teams have gone to bed and you have to wait until tomorrow for their judgements). I did a quick sketch in my diary to commemorate the occasion.

I'M SURE THEY SAID TRAGO MILLS WAS THIS WAY.....

We had another cause for concern over his delayed appearance as he had collapsed in the print works a few weeks earlier with, as far as I recall, some kind of haemorrhage and whisked to the county hospital, from where he discharged himself against doctors' advice two days later, turning up at the office on a Saturday morning to say "Hi." We asked him how he was. "Mighty fine," he replied, and carried on as if nothing had happened.

Polaroid palaver

For a time we had a Polaroid camera in the Packet's advertising department and were expected to go out and photograph sale houses for estate agents' copy or cars for the motors ads, whilst at the same time collecting advertising copy from those clients. It was a hit and miss affair.

We would point and click the 220 in the normal way and a print would momentarily emerge with a whirring sound from the interior of the heavy, grey plastic brick; we then had to "fix" each snap with a pungent liquid held by an absorbent canvas strip on a black plastic stick stored in a black plastic tube, without which the image would fade; and then we'd arrange the pictures across the dashboard to dry them out. What a palaver!

The stink would permeate the vehicle and you'd find yourself coughing and your eyes watering, so you'd have to wind down a window, even in winter and in the rain, to fend off impending unconsciousness. Often, as we whisked back to the office, a partly-dried print would flutter to the floor of our company Hillman Imps (especially if we had the window open or the air blower on) and the snap would immediately attract a layer of fluff and scurf from the grubby carpet.

If you didn't completely soak the image side of the print with fluid it would streak, and then fade in the streaks, so you didn't leave them on the office window ledge in the sun for too long! Oh, and the cameras broke down constantly (as did the Hillman Imps).

Christmas Dangles

I finally joined the newsroom and things changed yet again.

One year we decided to add to the seasonal cheer by hanging a load of Christmas decorations in the news room – but hanging *downwards*, instead of across the ceiling.

It was great fun, and crossing the room flicking aside the dozens of multi-coloured paper strips dangling like the beaded threads of a screen door was rather like being under the ocean, weaving a path through thin filaments of tinted seaweed.

Sadly it all had to come to an abrupt end due to the real prospect of a major fire. So the pretty streamers were relocated to hang in their proper position and no-one ever became briefly entangled, as suggested by my cartoon at the time.

XMAS in the
News Room
Meant streamers
hanging from the
Ceiling....

Course Shorthand

Oh, here's a footnote to my starting my news room career back in 1974.

When I joined I already had 110 words per minute shorthand: Pitmans, of course, and learned in a sporadically successful stint on a commercial course at Falmouth Technical College – and with the certificate to prove it. My editor at the time suggested I should have some light training, even though I'd made the transfer as "an adult entrant." This meant I wasn't a trainee on a training course; I was already an established staff member, drifting in from another department. Great, I thought: I'll get a crash course in law and subbing, both pretty useful if you want to be a relatively competent journalist.

"Now, what shall we do?" editor Roy asked, rhetorically. "I know! We'll send you on a shorthand course!"

This perceptive wheeze of his didn't last long – like about one session where the tutor, who appeared to know less about the subject than me and had at least a comparable writing speed, asked: "What the hell are *you* doing here?"

Some years later, on another paper, I tried to get myself attached to a rather excellent subbing course run by the National Union of Journalists, but the company wouldn't pay the fee and I couldn't afford it myself. They did offer to loan me to the subbing desk of one of the group's other papers for half a day a week, but seeing their subbing staff hardly had time to get their own work done each week it seemed pretty unlikely that they would welcome my glowing face, puffed up with eagerness to learn a new skill, loitering next to their jaundiced work stations. (Yes, I know a work station can't be jaundiced, but let me have a Lewis Carroll moment as you get the drift).

Latterly most of the trainees were learning Teeline shorthand, which was accepted by the National Council for the Training of Journalists and was regarded as quicker to grasp. I never ventured into this new territory, though I did like the short form for a phrase much-used in reportage "accident blackspot," which was an X followed by a dot!

As anyone who has ever attempted Pitman's shorthand will know, the system is comprised of straight lines, curves and circles, all imitating the sound of syllables. For instance, a short vertical line gives us the *t* sound, as in *tiny,* and a short horizontal line gives us the *k* sound as in *cat* or *kitten.* You master it by learning the symbols, the short forms that make the system quicker, and through reading printed shorthand exercises. In some cases the exercises pose questions.

During one of my early shorthand lessons at Falmouth Tech, students were reading a short piece of printed shorthand from a textbook when we came across a figure comprising a downward L, a horizontal G line, an S circle and a double-N which overall made the sound *L-G-S-N-dr*). One of my male colleagues (there were only two of us amongst the sea of perms) ventured: "Is it *legs-under?*" The tutor shook her head and, to much laughter, enunciated "AL-EX-ANDER. As in Alexander the Great."

I took great pedantic pains in pointing out that the G should have been a C, as the name was pronounced Ale*x*ander not Ale*g*sander. I was told the point was debatable, which is true, and the textbook version was the one to follow. And then I thought: How many secretaries are *ever* going to come across *Alexander the Great* in their daily dictation duties? Unless it's the name of their boss, I suppose, or they work in a museum.

Part 5
Your Side of the Ribbon

A very brief history of newspapers
Council stuff
Up before the beak
Oysters and mushrooms

A Very Brief History of Newspapers

I once bought an ancient copy of *The Times* in a second hand shop for £4. Dated Wednesday, June 23, 1858, the gradually yellowing but sturdy 16-page broadsheet contained a host of fascinating material from which I have selected just two. The first is a page one "small ad" for a public reading by a famous Victorian novelist, a reminder that Mr Dickens had a very public face in his time, much like an *X Factor* winner, though with greater talent and longevity. The second is a sobering report from America on page nine, published without additional comment, which shows that the Commonplace Unacceptable is only a few years back, tentacles of which still survive today.

MR. CHARLES DICKENS will READ at St. Martin's-hall, THIS AFTERNOON, June 23, at 3 o'clock, the Story of LITTLE DOMBEY ; and on To-morrow evening, June 24, at 8 o'clock, his Christmas Carol. Stalls, numbered and reserved, 5s. ; area and galleries, 2s. 6d. ; unreserved seats, 1s. Tickets to be had at Messrs. Chapman and Hall's, publishers, 193, Piccadilly ; and at St. Martin's-hall, Long-acre.

HIGH PRICES FOR NEGROES. — The *Casville* (Georgia) *Standard* says :—" On Tuesday last (sale day) the Negroes belonging to the estate of John Russell, deceased, were sold to the highest bidder. One man, about 20 years old, sold for $1,404 ; one 22 years old, $1,300 ; negro woman and two children, $1,450 ; boy, six years old, over $500 ; girl, seven years old, over $800 ; boy, 12 years old, $1,000 ; girl, 13 years old, $1,101. The rest of the Negroes sold for prices corresponding with the above. Terms eight months, with interest from date."

Though we now live in times where the typewriter is archaic and the traditional newspaper is said to be dying out – due to severe competition from 24 hour television "rolling news" coverage, the internet, and "citizen journalists" on such platforms as Facebook and Twitter – papers are still publishing (though many have fallen by the wayside).

So here is a brief rundown of the history of this mighty but flawed institution.

The first recorded newspaper is said to have been instigated by Julius Caesar. It was carved on stone or metal, called the *Acta Diurna* ("daily events") and was routinely posted in public places to report official political business and other matters of civil interest. It's amazing they had time for reading with all the debauchery and backstabbing prevalent around 130BCE (and now).

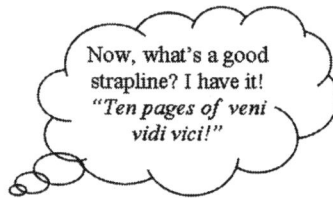

Now, what's a good strapline? I have it! *"Ten pages of veni vidi vici!"*

Manuscript newsletters were circulated in the late Middle Ages from various international traders, including the Fugger family, who were German merchants and bankers from Augsburg. The Fuggers were the richest family in Europe in the late 15th century and, in an early version of 20th century news barons, played a major role in arranging credit for the Hapsburg emperors, notably Charles V. It has been observed that newspapers have been run by a bunch of useless fuggers ever since. (Sorry about that).

The earliest-known news pamphlet in England was apparently an eyewitness account of the English victory over the Scots at the Battle of Rodden in 1513. Verbal forerunners of these single-topic information sheets were, of course, the town crier and the balladeer, and not forgetting the likes of "word of mouth" conveyance, bonfires and tribal drums, the forerunner of Twitter.

In 1563 the Venetians began producing news sheets to be read aloud to the public. The cost of admission to one of these readings was a small coin called a *gazeta* – and "gazette" became the common name for official news sheets, as opposed to "gazelle," which would only run about uncontrollably and probably end up poking you with a pointy horn.

The invention of printing allowed more conventional newspapers to develop and in the first two decades of the 17th century fairly regular papers printed from movable type appeared in Germany, Italy and the Netherlands. Single-page collections of news items from foreign journals, called *corantos* – the forerunners of modern newspapers – were circulated around this time by the Dutch, with English and French translations published in Amsterdam as early as 1620. Broadsheets with social news were published in Japan in the Tokugawa period (1603-1867) and the first English *corantos* appeared in London in 1621.

By 1645 there were around fourteen papers for sale in English in London including *Dillingham's Moderate Intelligencer*. The *Oxford Gazette* was founded in the year of the Great Plague of London, 1665 and that paper became the *London Gazette* one year later, the year of the Great Fire of London. So, at least two good front page lead stories there, then.

THE LONDON GAZETTE.

Published by Authority.

From Monday, Septemb 3, to Monday, Septemp 10, 1666.

Whitehall, Sept. 8.

THE ordinary course of this paper having been interrupted by a sad and lamentable accident of Fire lately happned in the City of *London*: it hath been thought fit for satisfying the minds of so many of His Majesties good Subjects who must needs be concerned for the Issue of so great an accident, to give this short, but true Accompt of it.

Church, neer Holborn-bridge, Pie-corner, Aldersgate, Cripple-gate, neer the lower end of *Coleman-street,* at the end of *Basin-hall-street* by the *Postern* at the upper end of *Bishopsgate-street* and *Leadenhall-street,* at the *Standard* in *Cornhill* at the church in *Fenchurch street,* neer *Cloth-workers Hall* in *Mincing-lane,* at the middle of *Mark-lane,* and at the *Tower-dock.*

On Thursday by the blessing of God it was wholly beat down and extinguished. But so as that Evening it unhappily burst out again a fresh at

The first American newspaper was the *Publick Occurrences Both Forreign and Domestick,* which was published in Boston in September 1690 – and suppressed by the colonial governor after one issue. Perhaps he was outraged by the miscellaneous spelling, or maybe they printed something dodgy about his mistress.

In 1704 a weekly *Boston Newsletter* was issued by the postmaster. Benjamin Franklin's brother James began *The Boston Gazette* in 1719 and the *New-England Courrant* in 1721. After several hiccoughs, Press freedom in the United States was won in 1791 and supported by the First Amendment to the US Constitution. Which probably meant more stories about prominent mistresses.

The first English daily newspaper was the *Daily Courrant*, which published from 1702-1735, and this was followed by a host of other titles, including *The Tatler* in 1709 and *The Examiner* (edited by novelist Jonathan Swift) in 1710. But it was not until 1771 that Parliament formally conceded the rights of journalists to report its proceedings – the same year the French published their first daily, *Journal de Paris*.

The *Daily Universal Register* was founded in England by John Walter in 1785 just two years after a peace treaty between Britain and America ended the American War of Independence. The *Register* became *The Times* three years later in 1788, a paper that between 1815 and the mid-19th century increased its circulation from 5,000 to 50,000.

In 1896 Alfred Harrnsworth (Lord Northcliffe) launched the *London Daily Mail* and introduced the first tabloid newspaper, the *Daily Mirror*, in 1930. This baby was half the size of its broadsheet parents at 15in x 23in. The first American tabloid was the *New York Daily News* of 1919, which was apparently devoted to sex and sensationalism but probably didn't have a Page Three model. Even the great broadsheet 'Thunderer' *The Times* eventually turned tabloid with its final broadsheet edition published on October 3, 2004.

People apparently fell in love with their newspapers.

Early in the 20th century American papers reached their peak with more than 2,000 dailies and 14,000 weeklies, and while these numbers soon declined circulation actually rose. At the close of the twentieth century, Europe had more than 2,600 dailies.

Due to the invention of the first practicable telegraph in 1835, news agencies came into being, further expanding the scope of reportage, the field becoming dominated by Reuters, the Associated Press, United Press International and Agence France-Presse.

The advent of the computer further revolutionised the newspaper and publishing industry by largely doing away with hot metal, manual typesetting, chemical photo processing – and, ironically, many of the very people who actually created it: its journalists and its printers.

Now you can also read your favourite newspaper electronically on the internet where world news is streamed continually on a vast array of constantly-updating web sites. And, as I said at the outset, you can also enjoy the imprecise ramblings of "citizen journalists" on a vast array of contemporary platforms, including mobile phone, PDA, laptop, tablet or Paddington.

Fortunately, the paper paper is still here! But only just...

Council Stuff – or "Is it on the Agenda?"

"Actually, you'd be surprised how many reporters attend our meetings these days with our new, sympathetic Press facilities..."

To begin this local government extravaganza, here's an actual report of mine from 1979, including the accompanying cartoon, which were published largely due to both the good humour of the council involved and the sub editor who often accepted my rather frivolous pieces as quite amusing.

It also serves to show the more spontaneous side of local town and parish councils: moments when they are not getting hot under the collar about litter, footpath management, dog fouling and political party bickering and can attend to those little, insignificant things.

Schadenfreude is not intended here, or in any of the following observations of civic life, though there are some examples that might encourage a small degree of pleasure at others' self-inflicted tribulations along the way.

GHOSTLY GOINGS ON IN THE HALL!

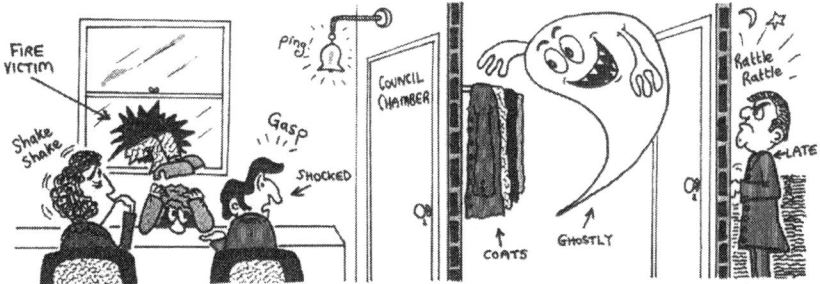

The Curse of the Phantom Doorbanger. A short novel starring members of Newton Abbot Town Council.

Chapter 1: A depleted group of town councillors, huddled together but several feet apart due to the sinister absence of some of their colleagues, hear the dread words of a minute from the house committee. The minute states that the leaving of coats in the hall of 2 St Paul's Road during a council meeting 'must be regarded as fair risk.'

Chapter 2: Coun Frank Birkett informs a hushed group that he had not been concerned about his coat until he read the minute... but now he is worried. The Mayor, Coun Mrs Frances Humpherson, says that the green front door of the council offices is the only exit in case of fire, and that the door cannot really be secured. Coun Birkett replies that 'it could be the only secure door for my coat."

Chapter 3: Members suggest that the door should be locked to protect the coats and their valuables. Strange noises of doors opening and closing have been heard in the hallway during council meetings. On investigation, no-one has been found skulking and no valuables missing. There are hushed references to ghosts.

Chapter 4: Members persist that the door should be locked, and that should there be a fire members could always 'jump out of the windows.'

Chapter 5: The point is raised that if the door is locked, as has been suggested, how are councillors who are late for the meeting to get in? No-one suggests by the window, but Coun David Prouse trots out to check that the front door bell is working. A dull tinkle fills the council chamber. Yes, the bell can be heard! Just.

Chapter 6: A happy ending. Members agree that the door should be locked – for an experimental period to protect the coats. There is much rejoicing.

Musicus interruptus

One town council I visited regularly for their 7pm monthly meetings assembled in a small ground floor council chamber equipped with a raised platform for the clerk and Mayor, a long rectangular horseshoe of tables for council members and a card table in the far corner for the Press represented by myself from the local weekly and a colleague from the evening paper. The ground floor chamber was just below a large community hall. On one balmy evening in the mid 1980s deliberations were suddenly interrupted in the following fashion whilst a member was on his feet speaking.

"Well, Mr Mayor (*thump*), I feel that (*yelp*) we should do something about (*clatter, crash, thump, bark*)..." The rest of the point was lost in the momentary melee.

It turned out the first floor hall had been hired out for a series of dog training classes which were all taking place on the very nights that the full council was meeting, hence the thumps and yelps.

Once the situation was explained members carried on their business as usual – as I wrote at the time "without a single comment or ceiling-ward glance. They must be well trained."

However, on another occasion members were less tolerant. The hall was alive with the sound of music one night – and it was definitely not one the council's favourite things.

The halls are alive with confounded muzak...

As the meeting progressed, the increasingly strident sounds of an electric organ seeped into the council chamber, distracting members from the civic matters at hand who were finding it increasingly difficult to concentrate.

Asked one councillor: "What is that sound of music coming through the ceiling?"

The clerk glanced briefly skywards and replied: "The Town Players."

"Only dog training classes are allowed to use the town hall during a full council meeting," the councillor responded.

As the melodious strains grew, another councillor offered to climb every mountain (well, at least negotiate the stairs to the hall) to investigate. He returned moments later, like the lonely goat herd, to report that the *do ray me* upstairs was indeed the local players rehearsing. They had been told they could have the hall all week with no restrictions but promised to keep the volume down and refrain from too much thumping.

Jusst a minnute...

Here's another piece culled from one of those delightful nights at the card table listening to happy chuntering into the late evening – or until members retreat into Part Two, the private section of the agenda when the Press are asked to leave. There are cries of *whoopee* as we stow our notebooks and hit the streets...

What is the *loosening of the celt*? Perhaps the letting-go of some ancient Gaulish kinsman, or the dislodging of some chisel-edged prehistoric instrument? This was the question to the answered for --- Town Council this week.

A withdrawn minute regarding the mayor's chain referred to *the condition of some of the plate and the loosening of the celt.*

Cllr Mrs W asked what the *celt* was.

Council clerk Mr F replied: "The minute has been withdrawn."

Cllr Mrs W: "I know that. I just wanted to know what it was."

Mr F: "It's a misprint."

Cllr Mrs W: "Yes, but what was it?"

Mr F: "It's supposed to be *link.*"

It was one of several entertaining "misprints" on the council's monthly agenda.

There was a tentative *enquirei*, a price to be *dislosed* and an invitation to *sig* a new agreement. A document was to be passed from member to *memeber* and flower tubs would, perhaps medievally, *brigyten* up part of a local close.

Members tittered on the question of *car mashing* outside the town hall (a difficult task when armed with only a chamois and bucket) and likewise giggled at the problems of *stining nettles* around the children's play area.

The council was also to buy *an hydraulic slef closing unti.*

However, each *meber* took in good part the making of a new lexicon and hoped that things would improve in time for the next *meeeting.*

Pause for celebration

A nearby parish council, on discovering in the middle of one of its meetings that a long-standing member was celebrating a special occasion, suspended standing orders and deliberations for several moments to collectively sing "happy birthday." No cake appeared.

Getting it right

From a county council agenda.

```
A motion was moved by Councillor S--- and duly
seconded:-
that the resolution to Education Committee Minute
305 be amended as follows:-
in sub-paragraph (a) (iv) by the deletion of
"Plymouth Girls High School" and the substitution
therefor (sic) of "Plymouth High School for
Girls".
```

Yes, I know it's the distinction between a school exclusively for Plymouth girls (incorrect) and a girls' school sited in Plymouth (correct). Even so, thoughts of sledgehammers and walnuts abound.

Flighty

A town council finance committee was interrupted one evening by a sudden unexpected cry, bringing discussions to a temporary halt. Everyone looked at a rapidly-blushing lady member, anxious to know what was wrong.

Cllr Mrs S (Conservative): Oooh!

Cllr Mrs N (Labour): What's the matter?

Cllr Mrs S (Conservative): A fly just went down my blouse.

Cllr H (*very* Liberal): It certainly knows where to go!

The blob that came out of the ceiling:
A town hall adventure

A brown stain, rather than a dark cloud, was hanging over the heads of town councillors. It stared down at them from the ceiling of their council chamber and was beginning to irritate the community's decision-makers.

It came under the microscopic scrutiny of the finance committee when members fell into a brown study over what to do with the unwelcome blob. They made it clear they wanted to see it eradicated somehow – perhaps with white paint, to match the rest of the ceiling.

Cllr M: I was told that if it was painted it would stick out like a sore thumb. But I would prefer a dirtyish white to a horrible brown stain.

But what caused the stain? Was it an upwardly mobile cup of tea, a leaking pipe, or something even more dastardly?

Cllr M (*mysteriously*): It was a chimney.

Cllr T (*spotting a cheap solution*): Are we hanging up Christmas decorations? You could hang a load of balloons over it.

Council clerk (*thinking of budget*): If it's painted the whole ceiling will need to be done.

Finance chairman (*likewise*): Let's patch it first and then see what it looks like.

Cllr S (*more so*): It's a waste of money to employ someone to do such a small job. I can pop in myself, with my own pot of paint.

The stain declined to comment.

Boxed in

One of the councils I reported on regularly had a large and long-winded clerk who was often at odds with his councillors. He would tower over them on a raised platform alongside the current Mayor and override many of their often rambling expositions. He also tended to create his own version of previous council discussions when making up the minutes, which tended to irk various long-serving members.

At a time when British Telecom was dispensing with most of its iconic red telephone boxes, especially in rural areas, the company wrote to the council offering to sell it one of the town's obsolete phone boxes for £100. This would allow the council to retain it as a monument or put it to some alternative community use once BT's telecommunications equipment was removed. Some other councils had gone ahead with the idea and one had even turned the 9ft x 3ft 4in space into a miniature book-swap library.

However, after a brief discussion the proposal was rejected by members, mainly because of the cost, but not before one of the supporters had suggested a future use.

"We could always put the clerk in it," she said.

Footnote. There is a UK company called Red Kiosk that refurbishes old British Telecom red telephone boxes, adding a power supply and leasing them out as 'retail pods,' often mini food and beverage kiosks, working alongside the Thinking Outside the Box charitable trust. The firm was set up in Brighton in 2014 by businessmen Eddie Ottewell and Steve Beeken.

Rural clients queue at rural phone box

Fireside

When a fondly-regarded, now departed district council chairman stood down in the 1980s, I presented him with this farewell card, which recorded both his casual, home-spun style and set out his most popular clichés in one drawing and two sentences.

"At the end of the day we are in a changing situation and, when the cards are on the table, we have to stand up and be counted - because, right from Day One, I had to be quite clear that, in this day and age, we had to get our act right. And I'm taking all that on board, Mr Prouse..."

Bump. Woof!

A district council chairman was giving a welcoming address at a charity horse racing night – not racing with real horses, of course; they were on film. He told the assembled throng: "And the proceeds from tonight will be going to the Blind Dogs for the Guides."

Election night spite

It was customary for reporters to gather at the district council offices to collate the local election results every four years and on one night the Press corps was especially delighted to hear that one particularly annoying councillor had lost his seat. There was even a small cheer.

Next thing, the guy was in the Press room, lounging drunkenly in one of the seats, spreading his repulsive fag-making paraphernalia over everything and puffing weedy little clouds of noxious nicotine gas into the previously unpolluted air (which was pretty rare for a Press room at that time). He started getting in the way, interfering with matters reporters were phoning as copy to their titles and distributing his personal brand of incorrect information to the gullible novices from two local radio stations.

When he was reminded it was a PRESS room, he said: "I'm only here because Jim Banter wants to see me."

A search for regional reporter Jim Banter found him phoning copy in another room.

"You want to see the happy loser?" he was asked.

"Do I hell!" Jim replied, and stayed where he was.

The unwanted ex-councillor was eventually ejected by council election staff, but not before he and his other half had engaged in a loud and bitter row across the Press table to add to their unwelcome presence.

Keeping it clear (as mud) 1

From a report on changes to the Devon County Structure Plan.

The panel noted that the HBF did not challenge the broad methodology of the county council's demographic projections.

Keeping it clear (as mud) 2

Constantly urged never to use jargon when writing, the bane of council reports, one reporter was surprised to receive a list of typed questions from the editor that his chief wanted his subordinate to ask about the rise in the number of planning appeals received in one year by the district council, which included the following:

7. Is there any correlation in the curve with the change of [the chief planning officer] to think-tank status?

From council minutes:

```
8-The Clerk is to ask Mr Coombes to look at the
cisterns of the bottom toilet and the ladies which
appear to be over-flowing very often.
```

I feel sorry for those overflowing ladies.

Quote in a report on domestic violence (which is unacceptable, even without the cannibalistic error).

According to a Harris opinion poll, 20 percent of all adults and 25 percent of all college educated adults feel that wife eating is perfectly proper.

A memo from the California Department of Food and Agriculture advising employees of health and safety issues during working hours: *Travel between floors by elevator only in buildings having elevators.*

When a local district council introduced plastic refuse bins with wheels a reader submitted a string of photographs and captions about how to use the new product, a replacement for the old-style steel dustbins and much kinder on refuse collectors' backs. One favourite image was a snap of the reader sitting in his new bin wearing a cheeky expression, the lid raised part-way behind his head and the legend: *A fall-out shelter.*

A council committee clerk rang the news-room one day in a bit of a sweat because he'd managed to send out a sub-committee agenda with a private report attached. The restricted report was, as it happens, innocuous enough to be described as dull. The clerk said he couldn't stop the paper using any material in the report now it was inadvertently public, but could I keep it low-key?

"Yes," I said. "I've kept it low-key. I've spiked it."

```
The Chairman assured Cllr W that 'rationalisation'
of the electrical switch in the kitchen would be
included in the electrical survey being organised
by the Town Clerk.
```

I would hate to see an irrational electrical switch!

Extracts from a town council's instructions for a public gathering of the Cornish Gorsedd in 1974, at times helpful, at times fanciful and impertinent.

On accessing the car park: *Those entering from Commercial Road turn left or right depending on which direction the car is travelling...*

Minibus: *Because the site has NO car park, and since the returning procession is uphill, a 12 seater minibus will be provided to take the Bards who require transport back to the Town Hall.*

Tuneful resting: *It is appreciated that some Bards may find it tiring to stand for an hour. Chairs will therefore be provided on the right hand side of the Men-Omborth (Dais) near the Harpist.*

Etiquette: *The Council wish to impress on all Bards that the Gorsedd Procession to and from the Circle is a public affair through the streets, and it must be both orderly and impressive. There must be no breaking ranks to chat with spectators.*

In a debate on how to stop pedestrians wandering across a new and busy stretch of dual carriageway, one district councillor suggested erecting "a 10,000-volt fence with the notice *Frying Tonight.*"

Some councillors' comments during meetings.

"The property is in the ownership of the owner."

"I suggest we don't ask anymore. I suggest we write and ask."

"I think someone should be there [at a crucial meeting] as a detergent."

"I'm sick of all these [high street] problems with these articulate lorries."

In a similar vein, some councillors and sometimes ordinary members of the public often confused the spontaneous with the confidential, in this way: they would sidle up to me, lean in close and confide, "Now *this* is off the cuff," when they clearly meant "Off the record." This would leave me with the leeway to decide how much damage to their career or social position I might cause if I quoted them by name dispensing this secretive morsel. A good way over the matter – short of correcting them – was to write my piece quoting them up to the point when their "off the cuff" snippet came into view, and then drop that into indirect speech, without attribution and the unspoken suggestion that the writer himself knew this to be true.

As American novelist Kurt Vonnegut might have said – *Hi ho.*

For want of somewhere permanent to assemble, parish councillors have been known to meet in village halls, public libraries, schools and even in members' homes on occasion. One parish council that regularly met in their village primary school assembly hall had to sit on chairs designed for eight-year-olds, which were less than accommodating for middle-aged adults, who tended to droop over the sides of the seats and wriggle about constantly trying to get comfortable. It was even worse for a reporter in a similar chair trying to get his knees under a desk apparently designed for an anorexic pixie in order to rest his notebook on the lid.

That's not the most uncomfortable it can get, though. I once sat at the piano in a draughty village hall, on a cold, hard piano stool, resting my notebook on the slippery varnish of its curved lid. It was a special parish meeting called to discuss some pressing local issue (the prospect of a large supermarket arriving in the community, I think) and the tiny venue was packed. I was lucky to get the piano seat! As the meeting droned on I longed to whip up the lid and play some discordant arpeggio.

I was most drawn to the parish clerk, sitting hunched on the end of a long trestle table next to the parish chairman and district planning officer – an elderly gent in a faded suit diligently noting down the night's deliberations in a large exercise book, head bent, biro in one hand and a continuous supply of cigarettes in the other. He would exchange them during brief lulls in conversation, light up, take a puff, and then lodge the replacement between two fingers – where it would sit, gradually burning down and forming a long coil of ash until it was stubbed out at the very last moment before flesh began to singe, to be replaced by another. I found it more fascinating than the actual debate, the result of which – *"not in our back yard, thank you, though the planners will probably grant it whatever we say"* – was a foregone conclusion.

Up Before the Beak

The kind of compassionate Magistrates you might find on the bench

Getting to the bottom of it

When I arrived in Newton Abbot I found there were scuds of incest and buggery cases (many of the latter in a local public toilet) and I began to wonder just what kind of place I'd arrived in! In one of the toilet tales, a hole had been drilled between cubicles... Which reminds me of the Fawlty Towers moment when Sybil tells Basil that if he must fondle a guest he should have the courtesy to be in the same room with her.

The police apparently stationed themselves in the roof space of this toilet in order to catch some of the chaps at it, so to speak, which prompted some ribald and amusing tales.

One of them involved an officer, who was spying through a hole in the ceiling, silently communicating that some "action" was taking place in the stall by furtively alerting a nearby colleague – who was set to jump down to the facilities below and intervene – by flicking him with a feather duster.

A little too friendly...

A Cornish court convened to hear a fairly innocuous case and when the bench was seated – on a raised platform above a large oak table containing the clerk of the court and a bevy of solicitors – the chairman noticed thatthe defendant was a long way back in the courtroom, sitting nervously on a small chair.

"Would you come forward, please," the chairman requested moderately, gesturing to the timorous man on the faraway chair.

The defendant got up, walked gingerly towards the magistrates – and sat down at the solicitors' table between two startled advocates.

Unable to resist a smile, the Chairman of the Bench said: "Ah, you've joined us now." And he motioned to the usher to guide the confused defendant, who had probably never been in a courtroom before and was dazed by it all, to the appropriate seat.

Not what you thought

Police officers reading evidence from their notebooks in court can be the source of amusement due to their inability, often for legal reasons, to deliver their lines in anything other than a well-enunciated but tedious monotone.

In the case of a man accused of exposing himself indecently in a public place, one copper took the stand, opened his black notebook and began reading in just this manner, and was doing pretty well until he reached this immortal line regarding the interview he had recorded with the defendent: "I said 'You took your penis out and began masturbating' and he replied 'No, I was not masturbating, I was just flicking it around...'"

Sub editor (*reading a court story*): How can you have a 19-year-old *youth*?

Reporter: Well, it depends on how old you are.

Joke by Northern trainee (*obviously prepared to laugh at his own, though I guess this could apply to any area in the UK or abroad that you feel a need to parody*): "What do you call a Northerner in a suit?"

All: "Dunno."

Trainee: "*The accused.*"

Here comes the warden

If there's one thing you can say about charges on a magistrates' court listing, they're customarily verbose and often only hint at the incident that prompted them – as in the case of this brace of charges set against one individual, each (then) attracting a maximum £400 fine.

At ----, did throw down in ---- Street in the open air and there left a polythene bag in such circumstances as to cause the defacement of --- Street by litter. Con to S.1 Litter Act, 1983.

At ---, did fail to give your name and address when so required by a Traffic Warden. Con to S.162(1) R.T.A. 1972 and the Function of the Traffic Wardens Order 1970.

Or, as you and I might say:

The accused returned to his car, which he had only left for a moment in order to (say) drop an important document through his bank's letterbox, to find "some little Hitler" slapping a parking ticket on his windscreen in one of those sticky-backed plastic folders which he whipped off in a momentary fury and threw on to the pavement in disgust, telling the person responsible just what he thought of him and then driving off, incandescent and incognito.

A colourful incident involving one of those parking enforcers we love to hate took place some years ago in a seaside town. An especially punctilious warden made the misjudgement of placing a parking ticket on the vehicle belonging to a Chinese restaurant employee that was parked outside his place of work. The car's owner, who worked in the kitchens, was so enraged that he proceeded to chase the warden down the street, screaming at him in Cantonese and brandishing a meat cleaver over his head. Needless to say, his charge sheet bore slightly different wording...

Motorist's Revenge.
"What was that about a ticket, old boy?"

The policeman told a court that the man accused of drunkenness "was unsteady on his feet and his eyes were glazed." With that, the defendant removed one eye saying: "It was bound to be glazed." He was given a conditional discharge.

The legal profession is not always all it could be. Here's the body of a letter sent to the News Editor from a London-based solicitors:

Dear Sir,

Re: R.L.T—

We enclose new report with two documents to confirm and reply paid envelope to enable you to be so kind as to let us have a cutting of the report from your letter containing it.

Yours faithfully...

Oh, and the envelope contained just the above letter – alone, unappended, and only of itself, so help me God...

Having been alerted to this book, my chum Mike Truscott told me about a case he covered at Falmouth Magistrates Court way back in the dim past, between 1960 and 1980. Mike relates:

"The Clerk to the Magistrates in those days was a very authoritative guy who ruled the place like some sort of mini-God. Accordingly, he had a commanding, booming, no-nonsense, humour-free VOICE. Into the dock came the latest defendant (and how clearly I can still see the poor lad's straight face). [The clerk] duly read out the charge, without any kind of deviation, emphasis or implied comment, viz: 'It is said that at *such-and-such* a farm, on *such-and-such* a date, YOU DID COMMIT BUGGERY WITH A COW. How do you plead?'

"We, on the press bench, did NOT fall about laughing . . . purely because we had already seen this on the printed charge schedule which, of course, we always had in advance. But it was still a very close-run thing; we had the devil's own job keeping straight faces and preventing ourselves from falling out of our chairs, watching the faces of clerk and defendant for any sign, none forthcoming, of a lapse in emotional control."

Quite a moos story...

For my own court reminiscence, there was one over-enthusiastic reporter who would constantly comment on cases from the Press bench, while they were being heard. Brian Blessed-loud comments of the ilk "He looks guilty" (and before any evidence had been called) or "They should string him up," or personal remarks about the witnesses, magistrates, solicitors, members of the public, even the Chairman of the Bench (not wise). In fact, so much so that he was actually removed from the court room on several occasions for disrespectful behaviour, but still kept bouncing back.

A load of pants

A newly-arrived trainee thought she had done a pretty good job of reporting a minor case on one of her first assignments at the local magistrates' court. She wrote a straightforward account of one woman's legal unfortunates, filed the story and thought no more about it. Not, at least, until a report of the same case appeared in a rival newspaper.

The competitor story claimed that the defendant had been so irked with magistrates that she tore off her knickers and hurled them over the dock. This caused the trainee's editor to adopt the colour of a modest beetroot. Rightly concerned about this serious omission from the report by his youngest member of staff, he tackled her about the matter.

"It never happened!" she told him.

But the other reporter has said it did, was the reply.

"I should know," the by-now equally flushed trainee responded. "She was right in front of me!"

The editor persisted, as he had seen the same story in the *Daily Mirror*.

"Well," the now irate trainee barked. "You don't mean to tell me you believe everything you read in *The Mirror*?!"

And, stuffing a pair of court-soiled knickers into her handbag, she stalked off to find someone else to harass.

The above sentence here is my fictional ending. The final truth of the matter was never established as the other reporter also maintained that it *did* happen. Whatever the case, the knicker-flicker made a better story, even if its veracity was a matter of debate.

Oysters and Mushrooms: Won't You Join the Dance?

It was one of those culinary events that Edwin the Editor just *had* to have covered. After all, it involved a popular local college where he was great chums with the Principal – and one of his Rotary Club contacts had told him about it.

His REAL interest (also a Rotarian tip) was a plan to research the growth of Japanese mushrooms – called Shiitake (pronounced *she-tar-kee*, and not shit-ache, which is as good a description of the Pursuits of Edwin as any other at a time like this). But more of that heady aspect later.

Reporter Adrian – being an enthusiastic and obliging sort – was seconded to attend a select gastronomic festival for committed gourmets at this august establishment. It was on a Friday night and during the festivities, which involved a whole gamut of unusual food offerings, Adrian was offered an oyster. His story begins when he is approached by an unknown man we shall call *Man From Fish Farm* and proceeded thus.

Man From Fish Farm: Do you want to try an oyster?

Adrian (*not so enthusiastic...*): Er...

Newspaper photographer Cary Grantham: Go on, Adrian!

Adrian (*...but still obliging*): Oh, all right. [Munch munch]. Ugh. I hope it was dead.

Man From Fish Farm: Well, it is now...

Adrian (the *following Monday, centre-stage in the office*): "I thought it was a bit funny when he bent down and opened this box under the table that was full of water and seaweed..."

Anyway, Adrian collapsed at home in the early hours of Saturday morning, breaking his two false front teeth again (he broke them a few weeks before in another unforeseen incident) as he slumped dizzyingly to the floor. He was very ill all weekend and confined to bed. His doctor diagnosed food poisoning and singled out the under-the-counter shellfish. Adrian was also told that he would get recurring symptoms (hence the cartoon) and subsequently, every time he made an error his colleagues would nod sagely and say: "It's the oysters."

The story probably did nothing to decrease Edwin's credibility with the college as he now proceeded to fall over backwards to print every spit and cough about the place, to make up for the "regrettable incident" (mainly regrettable because we reported it). As one of the college staff muttered darkly to Adrian as he investigated the poisoning tale: "That'll never get in the paper – considering where it came from."

But, give Edwin his due, it did – and in some detail as well, with the front page headline FOOD POISONING PROBE. Even Edwin didn't like one of his own being subjected to the Crippen touch, no matter how inadvertently.

Anyway, to get back to the associated Shiitake Incident.

Edwin's Rotary contact had told him about the new horticultural plan and he asked Adrian and Cary to respectively interview and photograph the bods concerned at this fated gourmet do.

They get the story (before Adrian's introduction to a mouldy mollusc), but the growers don't want to be photographed. Instead they give Adrian a picture of the mushrooms and a fuzzy picture of themselves. Adrian and Cary decide the picture won't reproduce, so they hand back the mug shot and take the mushroom shot.

On the following Monday Edwin, dissatisfied with this arrangement, gets Adrian to ring the growers and get the declined photograph dropped off at the paper. This occurs and Edwin sees for himself that the picture is unusable.

So he gets Adrian to call them back and fix up a time for Cary to return and take a picture of them both, with the logs in question and the mushrooms in question growing on them.

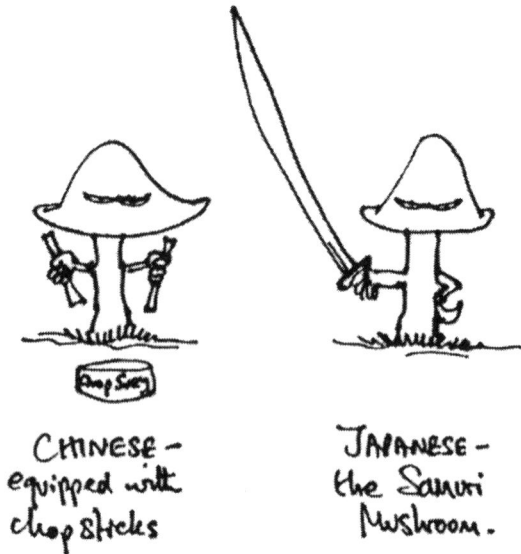

CHINESE –
equipped with
chop sticks

JAPANESE –
the Samuri
Mushroom.

The difference between Chinese and Japanese mushrooms

The visit is fixed, and Cary arrives only to be told by the shiitake crew: "There are no mushrooms on the logs. We haven't grown them yet."

Cary telephones Edwin and tells him this. But the fact that the very thing that Edwin wants photographed does not yet exist does not deter this formidable news-hound. He tells Cary to take a picture of the growers with their logs – as the logs are POTENTIAL mushroom-bearing logs. Cary rings off and goes back to the beleaguered duo, who by now are wishing they had never thought about growing effing Japanese mushrooms and would the bloody paper just shiitake off.

"Why have you got to have a picture of us, anyway?" asks one.

"Because the editor heard about it from one of his Rotary buddies," replies Cary bluntly, about as hacked off as the growers after making two trips to get the same picture.

The duo adopt that look of "Oh, THAT explains it," sympathise with Cary, pose as best they can with a set of denuded logs, and wave our cheery photographer off the premises.

The photo caption revealed that the prospective cultivators were shown "with some of the logs on which they hope to grow Japanese mushrooms..."

We never heard from them again.

Footnote. The reason these tips were often treated derisorily by reporters was that they were sometimes pretty useless and many times dispensed by members who seemed to want to ridicule our boss (only we were allowed to do that), who was in many respects a far better man.

Part 6

Our Side of the Ribbon

Animals, pets and pests
The desk saga
Parking perturbations
Hearts a flutter
Dictates

Animals, Pets and Pests
Ant with your coffee?

The hot drinks machine was set in an alcove in a corridor, sensitively positioned just outside the Ladies' lavatory, and was the size of a small wardrobe. It served up an indifferent coffee, a bitter tea and a strange concoction advertised as soup but looking more like cat sick. The powdered versions of these delicacies, along with powdered milk and sugar, were stored in the belly of the beast in metal containers, along with a water tank and a hideous red plastic bucket at the bottom to catch the drips and usually at least half full with slops.

If this wasn't a sufficient health hazard, each summer the machine became infested with ants – a kind-of annual mandible-mash for all social hymenopterans, a miniature Woodstock-style gathering but without the music or ticket touts. You could often see a line of them proceeding resolutely across the newsroom like a party of explorers on route for their El Dorado.

The year before the ghastly, rusty object was finally scrapped a carpet of ant powder was spread over the floor and nearby work surface by Edwin the Editor. Though he claimed the contrary, the machine had not been cleaned out properly in an age and there were dozens of the little black scuttlers crawling about and attempting their version of the breast-stroke in the water tank. Even his deputy was concerned about ant powder being liberally sprinkled over the one foot square shelf where cups were placed and filled.

Then the chief reporter added a wasted two pence worth: "It's not healthy, you know. People use that work surface. What if the poison gets in their drinks?"

"It won't do that," Edwin replied, with scientific certainty. "And it's not poisonous to humans."

"It kills ants."

"Exactly."

And, with the Gospel According to St Edwin of ANTioche, that was the end of that.

To be fair, no-one was actually poisoned (as far as I know). But that probably had more to do with the fact that pretty well everyone (except Edwin) stopped using the machine – and Edwin didn't collapse into a whimpering foetal ball, and he drank gallons of the stuff.

A short while after the ant contamination, and the only marginally successful sprinkling of death dust all over the insides of the machine, a man arrived unexpectedly to clean it out. He was snorting and grumbling and intimating that the rusted old hulk hadn't seen the right side of a squeegee in several decades when out popped the editor, as chirpy as a new spring dawn and the archetypal anathema to a low paid and beleaguered drinks machine cleaner.

Editor (*brightly*): Ah, that looks sparkling. How are you cleaning that?

Repairman (*icily and with meaning*): Soap and water.

On one occasion there was a shortage of clean coffee cups, no doubt because somebody forgot to order any. The thin white polystyrene containers came in cellophane tubes of about a hundred and there was usually at least one tube on the tiny shelf by the machine. Anyway, the editor, presumably with nothing better to do, set off on a hunt for coffee cups. He made a round of the offices collecting all the *used* plastic cups from desk tops and waste bins and piled *them* next to the coffee machine, unwashed. I don't think there were many takers...

Mind you, Edwin was always first on the scene if anything went wrong, though he often possessed no skills whatsoever to bring to the scenario, with the exception of keenness, kindness and an overarching need to save the firm money, as in the case of office furniture.

On another occasion the troublesome new telephone system crashed yet again and staff found they were unable to make outgoing calls. Instead of contacting the phone company immediately, to at least save time, subs Tom and Sam and Ad Manager Clarence waited for an hour for the sage advice of Edwin who arrived at 10am. He immediately grabbed a spanner from his tool kit and disappeared. Several minutes later receptionist Harriett appeared in the newsroom looking ruffled.

"I can't do any work," she complained. "He's got both desks out and is scrabbling about under them on the floor."

Mercifully, British Telecom was called soon afterwards.

Rats in the Skirting

Editor sets off on a wild beast hunt

As the above tales indicate, Edwin was never one to shirk getting his sleeves rolled up and involving himself in any project, no matter how small, though none of them bore any resemblance to what he should have been doing, i.e. subbing his paper.

One day, after a suspicious scuttling had been heard coming from the skirting boards, Edwin went on a Big Game hunt, searching for rats, which prompted the above cartoon. He spent some time on his hands and knees knocking the walls, though he was only armed (if memory serves) with a 12in plastic ruler. His hunt was abandoned without incident and exterminators eventually summoned. It was probably field mice.

Combustible Felines

An unexplained story idea found scribbled on a reporter's personal list – *heat-seeking kittens* – prompts cartoon.
BRITAIN'S NEW DETERRENT: IBM'S HEAT-SEEKING KITTEN RANGE OF MISSILES.

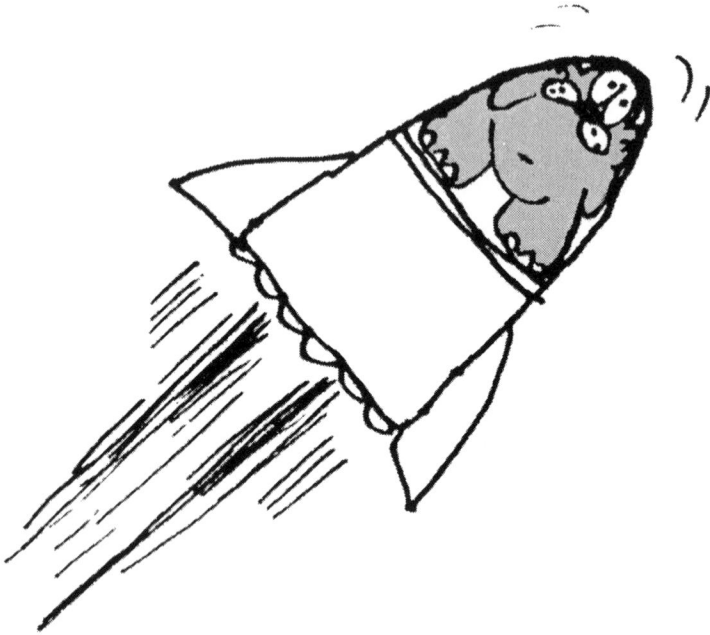

Thinking along the same lines...

Reporter Adrian received a call from the Cats Protection League asking for publicity because a number of cats were "disappearing from their homes" and there was a concern that vivisectionists might be on the prowl.

The first question Adrian asked was: "And is this the time of the year that cats usually go off?"

And the resultant quickie sketch below was, as they say, a given...

Name that pet

A bullock got loose and ran on to a neighbouring business premises, but when the manager rang in to tell the paper one of the two photographers was on a day off and the other was out on an Advertising assignment.

Trainee Whitney: "That's typical – get a good news picture and there are no photographers in."

The police eventually had to shoot the beast, and Adrian rang the station for details.

Adrian: "I'm ringing about the shooting of the bullock yesterday. Who do I speak to?"

Whitney (*a fistful of facetiousness*): "Sergeant Eastwood..."

After the call Adrian said the police were "playing down the incident because they had to shoot the bullock six times and made a bit of a mess of it."

Chief reporter Beeno: "Said a police spokesman, 'The bull, whose name after officers had shot it, was Colander...'

Coo coo... cough

One town council debated gassing the pigeons nesting in the roof of the town hall because their incessant cooing was upsetting the local drama group, which used the hall periodically. It led to this cartoon. I thought it would be nice if the pigeons were perceptive enough to know what was happening and decide to cluster, unseen, on the WWII ARP helmet of the prospective poisoner.

Whitney (*bashing out a tale about rats and pigeons breeding under the town in a river culvert and looking for a collective noun*): What do you call a group of pigeons?

Reporter Teebone (*darkly*): A bloody nuisance.

Whilst on the subject of pigeons – a bane of local authorities due to their congregation on public buildings and their indiscriminate splattering of pavements and pedestrians below – they are often considered to be the stupidest of birds. I spied one of these grey loons on a fishbone television aerial in a heavy rain storm.

It was flexing its wings, like it was in a power shower (which it was), in order to wash away various bugs and parasites that burrowed into its feathers. Which was fairly smart, I thought. A few days later I saw what may have been the same pigeon on the same aerial undertaking the same manoeuvres – only this time it was in a furious hail storm. I guessed it just wanted to knock its pestilent unwanted resident unconscious so they'd drop out, stunned.

Teebone (*putting his coat on*): "I'm going to see a woman about a cat."
  Beeno: "She lives in a mews, does she?"

One of the reporters was told about a local lady who had a lively dog that hated people coming to the house so, in an attempt to restrain it, she put double glazing on the front door. One day the dog was at the top of the stairs when a caller rang the bell. The dog catapulted down the stairs... and crashed straight through the double glazing. Final touch: the caller was a double glazing salesman.

Line in a village correspondant's report: *The high spot of the day was the prestigious duck race.*

The Desk Saga

The move was nothing like this...

It is a pleasant, unassuming Wednesday when advertising manager Clarence Mildly strides into the news room with Edwin the Editor, demanding the short-term loan of a desk.

Ed readily says he will comply and peers about the collection. There are around a dozen timber desks in the office, all of them very old and decrepit, with everyone having the use of at least two, the first for typewriter, in/out trays, telephone books and other day-to-day paraphernalia, and the second for various piles of ancillary this-and-that (mostly rubbish that no-one can be fagged to throw away). Each twin set is closely guarded by their occupants, much like a battle-hardened front line squaddie defends his precious, self-dug foxhole from unwanted interlopers.

Ed (*to Clarence*): "How about this one?"

He points to a former trainee's desk inside the external door. It is currently unoccupied as said trainee is now an ex-trainee, having left the fold for places new. However.

Chief Beeno (*foolishly interrupting*): "You can't take that one. Terry Mote is joining us on Monday, that's where he's going to sit and I'm not having him arrive to find there's no desk for him."

Ed (*who knows this, having personally employed Mote*): "Oh, that's Monday, is it? Well, we'll look elsewhere."

Beeno (*taking an unwarranted Mothercare-style interest in the office furniture*): "We haven't got a spare desk. All our desks are being used.

How long are we loaning it for?"

Ed: "Pro tem."

Beeno: "And how long's that?"

Ed shrugs, Clarence says "Well, you sort it out" and exits.

After a brief but fractious argument between editor and chief reporter, Edwin stalks over to reporter Adrian's desk. Adrian has a main desk, with another shoved in on its left hand side and pushed up against another reporter's desk to give them a partly-shared work surface. All the drawers and most of the working area are littered with Adrian's detritus. Ed ponders.

Ed: "Which of these would you prefer to use?"

A moment later Adrian begins hopping about like a pet spaniel, emptying the drawers of the larger desk in preparation for its removal to Advertising, just down the corridor. There then follows one of those priceless in-office jazz dances.

Removals Part One:
Multi-movement installation for office furniture and lackeys

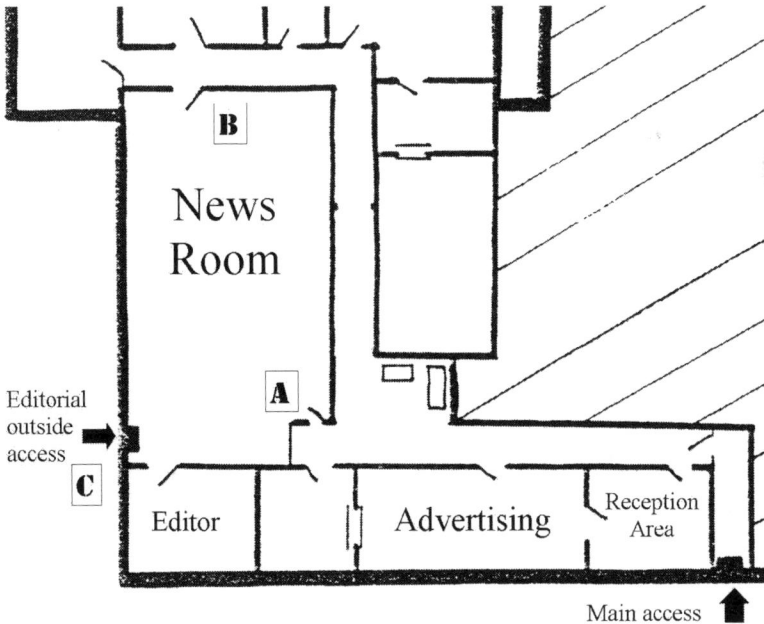

B

News
Room

Editorial
outside
access

A

C

Editor

Advertising

Reception
Area

Main access

In order to fully appreciate the scale and setting of the following frolic, some understanding of the layout of the "stage" is required. The news room is a large, rectangular space with desks arranged (chucked in) on both sides with a wide walkway between them, down the middle of the room.

At the bottom end of the room there are three doors: extreme right is the nearest door to Advertising (A), accessing a narrow corridor; to its right is the door to the Editor's office and, next to that, sited in the exterior wall, is the exit door to the outside world and freedom (C). The corridor that serves all the various offices runs around the top and right side of the news room and a further door to this corridor is situated in the centre of the far newsroom wall (B) between two huge notice boards.

Picture a busy but small newsroom. Day. Subs Tom Sears and Sam Trafford sit dumbly at their desks, as does Beeno, who is simmering quietly. At this point, please consult your helpful diagram on the previous page.

Ed and Adrian upend Adrian's fated desk, now cleared of its contents, and carry it to the door facing the part of the surrounding corridor nearest to advertising (*door A*). Sam, being nearest politely stands and opens the door with the feigned air of an obsequious butler. Adrian and Ed lift desk. The timber pens flap falls out with a crash. Sam picks it up. The impromptu removal men then try to get the desk out on its side – the side with the legs facing Ed's office. This fails. They back in and turn the desk the other way round, with the legs facing the corridor. This also fails. A struggle to get it through upright also meets with no success. They then hit on going through the corridor access at the other end of the office (*door B*).

They grunt and puff across the office as the desk is now getting fairly heavy and both men are of frail build. They try the same technique on door B as they tried before at door A, and, on the second swing, get the desk through. They are now heard grunting and banging up the corridor to the right and around the bend – only to come to a halt half way, stuck between two door jambs. They have forgotten about the disused frame that sticks out into the walking space at this point, left behind when an obsolete door was removed some years earlier.

They return to the news room in reverse with much more in the way of sound effects, struggle across the office and hit on the idea of – yes, you've guessed it! – door C: editorial's direct route to the outside world. Ed grips the outside door and forces it back so far that it scores the linoleum floor and almost ruptures the hinges and he and Adrian launch off again, narrowly missing the back of Ed's car, parked outside.

They carry the desk off down the front of the building, briefly enjoying the fresh air and avoiding potholes and parked vehicles, and finally bump up the short step and in through the front door. When they get to the second advertising door the desk gets jammed again and its extraction is accompanied by many bird-like calls, along the lines of "out again"..."no, take it down here"... "this way," etcetera, for some minutes.

The desk is eventually fitted in its new resting place – not for a member of staff, though, but for advertising rubbish overflow...

Removals Part Two:
Second furniture installation with ancillary carpentry
and part one finale

It is Friday of the same week when Head Office telephones.

A voice in Beeno's ear announces: "We've got these two gash desks from another office for your Ad department. Is anyone going to be there tomorrow to open up so that we can drop them off?"

Beeno hands the phone to Clarence. "Oh, no," Clarence says, trying to avoid a Saturday job and instantly dispelling any thoughts that the need for his desks is urgent, and rearranges delivery.

On Tuesday afternoon the long-awaited desks arrive after a 30 mile trip. There are two of them, metal and each weighing half a ton. They are delivered in a small truck by a driver who looks too old to lift a moderate-sized bar stool and he is accompanied by his pre-pubescent niece, who clearly is not in the furniture business. They wait while Sam the sub, who is first on the scene, scratches his scalp with concern, firstly standing on the parking strip outside the front door, then poking his head into the van before returning to the safety of the roadside.

By the time fellow sub Tom, newly-arrived trainee Terry Mote and Beeno arrive on the scene, Sam has begun complaining, wavering and generally getting the "who's this idiot?" look from both occupants of the van. Whatever his solo dance is in aid of – probably the scattering of panic – it achieves nothing. He scratches his head again at the sight of the arriving trio. Tom sympathises, as is his wont, and scratches his head too.

At this point, Beeno helpfully comments: "Bloody hell, we're not even going to be able to lift those down off the van, let alone get them down the corridor."

In the meantime trainee Terry Mote has recognised one of the desks as his old newsroom desk from another branch office; he hops on to the van and starts cooing at it, as if being reunited with an old girlfriend. Tom Sears, more constructively, suggests that at least we'd better get the desks out of the van and on to the ground.

Beeno decides to let Tom and Sam do the lifting, citing hastily-concocted Union regulations that (a) he does not want to totally incapacitate his spine and (b) "if the company wants bloody great four-ton desks wheeled about they should get proper removal men. I can just see the chief executive lugging them." This is not helpful.

Still, the team eventually get the two grey, steel monstrosities down and into the entrance corridor, blocking the access to both the newspaper offices and the adjoining office block. The van driver and his diminutive now helpfully abandon the project and drive off. Tom looks at Beeno; to be helpful, Beeno looks back. To be even more helpful, he looks at the desks, then at the door to the corridor and their goal, the advertising office, and observes: "They're not going to go through."

With a struggle the first desk is manoeuvred on to its side. It is two inches too deep. "Will the legs unscrew?" asks Tom, hopefully. Sam is still hovering and Terry Mote is scooping old papers from the inner depths of his former office appendage, perhaps in the hope of finding an unsubmitted expenses claim.

At this point tele-sales girl Mary arrives, wanting to get in to the ad office. Rather than walk back down the front of the building and in through the news room, she climbs over the second desk and in through a narrow glass-partitioned service hatch in the entranceway and on to the reception desk below. There is much cheering and cries of "be careful" from Advertising, whose members do nothing to aid the progress (or lack of it) of *their* desks.

It is at this sorry stage that Beeno suggests removing the door. Sam (who later claims responsibility for this idea), hops off to get his tool kit from the car. It proves insubstantial, and Beeno has to go and get his. He thinks about using it on Sam.

Whoever painted the doors last time round also painted over the slots in the screw heads and they start to annoy Sam "I am really Barry Bucknell" Trafford, who looks in danger of impaling his hand with the screwdriver. Trainee Terry appears rooted to the spot and Tom Sears is chattering away to the Ad girls about not very much.

Eventually the door is removed and dragged down to the end of the corridor like a coffin lid and the desks gradually progress with hefty pushing up to the Ad office door next to an old file room (now Clarence's office). It will not open because there is a filing cabinet behind it. Beeno asks the Ad girls – who are still standing around doing nothing but now compounding their lack of assistance by actually starting to give advice – to make themselves useful and move the item. They do so, with the kind of random disorganisation which makes the makeshift editorial removers look like international professionals from Pickfords.

At this point Beeno realises that the deputy Ad manager wants one of the new desks in the same location as that currently occupied by the purloined wooden newsroom loaner. "Oh, we'll take that back, then," he says, with no room for any argument. "We'd better get it out first.'

Tom looks at Beeno with that "You can't, because the corridor to the front door is blocked with two flaming great metal desks" look. But Beeno has already upended Adrian's old desk and realises that it will fit through the Ad door (*bottom of plan*, if you are still conscious at this point in the story) by just sliding it forwards and turning. It goes through clean as a whistle, with about an inch to spare on either side. It progresses equally easily down to the editorial door and straight through. Tom looks at Beeno as if he has just produced a bevy of doves from his jumper.

"I've brought your desk back, Adrian," Beeno says.

Ungratefully, Adrian (alone in the newsroom) snorts: "I'm manning the office while you're all out there playing around."

The team go back, move the two new desks in, drawers out, put them in place, reassemble them and leave. Sam and Beeno put the door back on.

Beeno: "Well, that wasn't too difficult, was it?"

Tom: "The editor wasn't here to organise it."

Footnote: Despite the urgency and commotion of demanding an editorial desk, the advertising department only had it for three and a half days and during that time no-one sat at it. A few bits of paper and art books were spread across its work surface. It looked happy back with Adrian, who immediately refilled it with all his junk.

Parking perturbations

Act I: Mine!

Monday. Clarence storms into the newsroom and soars to Beeno's desk like a man possessed. His ears are steaming. Perhaps he has had to do some work for a change, Beeno thinks, as our Clarence is not noted for over-stretching himself.

Clarence: "Your car is in my space."

Beeno (*who has parked on the corner of the building at a direct right-angle to the editor's corner slot*): "Pardon?"

Clarence: "That's my space. I don't want you parking in it."

Beeno: "There are no marked spaces here."

Clarence: "I'm not interested in that. That's my space. If you want to park at the front, park in Edwin's space and argue the toss with him."

(*Clarence exits swiftly, greatly piqued, before response can be given or Beeno's grunt of disdain can be heard. The door does not bang, being fitted with hydraulic dampers that allow it to languidly glide shut and ruining the effect of a good tantrum*).

Tuesday. Beeno arrives at work to find second photographer Cary Grantham parked in Clarence's spot, so Beeno parks in front of Cary.

Clarence arrives, blocks Cary in by parking right on his bumper and when Cary asks him to move so that he can go out on a job Clarence starts barracking him in the same agitated vein.

Eventually the red-faced photographer is released into the wild.

Wednesday. All quiet on the parking front. Sighs of relief abound.

Thursday. Beeno arrives to find Clarence parked one space up and parks behind him. No recriminations follow.

Friday. Volatile chief photographer Roly Hill parks in the space Clarence has claimed as his own. Unsurprisingly, no-one says a word, apparently unwilling to trigger Roly's wrath.

Act II: Mine Too!

While on holiday, sub-editor Sam Trafford has his favoured parking space just below editorial's main window purloined by his senior colleague Tom Sears, who continues to park there on Sam's return. Sam is most put out and complains to Editor Edwin. Edwin apparently tells Sam that there are no marked parking spaces, so (more or less) tough turkey.

The next day, in a fit of rare bravado, Sam decides to park in Edwin's coveted spot outside his own office window. To Sam's annoyance, Edwin arrives as usual, says nothing, and continues to say nothing about the incident all day, thus sidestepping any confrontations.

The following morning, Sam does the same again. This time he gets the anticipated response. After much driving around the building looking more and more miffed and gripping his steering wheel like a tug-of-war contestant, Edwin pulls up outside the office door and hops out, double parked and flings open the news room door. With editor silhouetted in the doorway and sub-editor rooted stiff-backed behind his desk the following mini-drama transpires.

Edwin: "Sam, can you move your car?"

Sam: "No."

Edwin: "Come along, Sam."

Sam: "No."

Edwin: "Sam, I want to park."

Sam: "Tough."

Edwin: "It was funny last week, Sam, but not this morning. Will you please move your car!"

The latter remark is not a question.

Sam: "No. There's nowhere else to park."

Edwin (*sounding like a scout master*): "We'll find a spot. Come on."

Sam unenthusiastically relents, goes to the door and exits, closing the door.

Through the office window Edwin and Sam are seen talking animatedly. They are joined by a mechanic from the nearby garage and there is much pointing of arms and revolving of heads. The mechanic and Edwin go off together. Sam returns to his desk and sits there looking determined. No subbing takes place.

One minute elapses before Edwin returns to his offstage position in the doorway.

Edwin: "I'm having that green car moved, so there will be a space."

Sam: "Well, park in it, then!"

Edwin exits, there is a protracted pause and then Sam wanders out muttering. He moves his car and returns in the same vein while Edwin, smiling the satisfied smile of a darts player who has just hit *one hundred and EIGHTY*, parks in his usual spot.

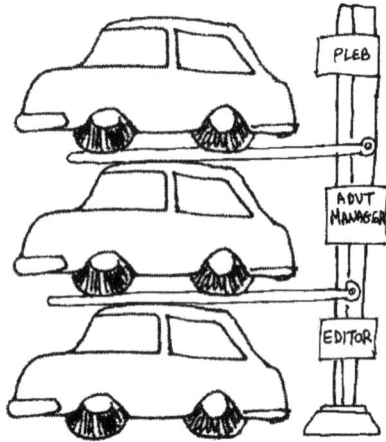

A possible solution to the problem

Act III: Ours!

In order to transform a cupboard used as a file room into an office for two, the company decides to have all the old newspapers, bound in yearly volumes, moved to some new offices a half-mile away.

For this task they employ a couple of seedy-looking Herberts who would not have looked out of place in *The Sweeny*. The dubious duo arrive on a Friday morning with a large truck, which they park slant-wise outside Edwin's office, his car not being parked in its hard-won spot on this occasion; this effectively blocks all access and egress to and from the busy industrial yard at the back. They begin loading files with much banter, most of it shouted the full length of the busy news room as they tramp between "cupboard" and truck, as they are using Editorial as a walk-through, its outside door jammed open to accommodate the task.

Herbert and Herbert toss the bound files into the back of their vehicle as if they are bags of builders' waste with little or no regard for their ancient and fragile nature and make it almost impossible for reporters and subs to do any phone business due to the racket. Then the crunch: they have finished, they are fully loaded, they clap hands together to dust them off... only to find they can't go anywhere because they have a flat tyre. And no spare.

Herbert One gets Sam to dial their depot as he can't understand the newspaper's phone system. Surprisingly Sam does not make some comment along the lines of "you stick your finger in the holes..." Meanwhile Herbert Two wanders off outside as if seeking heavenly intervention.

Eventually both of them disappear in the general direction of the town centre, leaving the lorry where it is and causing garage mechanics to hop up and down with frustration as nobody can get around it.

The lorry is still parked there at teatime...

Footnote: The next day Editorial was told that the old files – constantly referenced by reporters – were "no longer available." They had reached the new office, we were told, but nobody had had a chance to sort them out. There were expressions of hope that those newly-entrusted with the area's history would at least be able to get the years in the right order.

Commented Sam: "They should all be put on microfilm, anyway..." They never were.

Hearts a-Flutter

Merry Valentine recipient (though not a mayor or nurse)

One year, my editor decided it would be a nice gesture for the paper to present the current town mayor with a Valentine's card to mark the sterling work she was doing for the community.

This was one of those gestures designed to show the paper's interaction with the community it served, but may also have been devised because the next issue was due to publish on February 14, Valentine's Day.

The idea was sound enough in itself, but the whole thing became a bit of a pantomime – or, as my parody of the incident at the time chose to portray it, it bit of a ballet.

The Valentine
(A Ballet)
Choreography – Edwin the Editor
Music – Everybody else

Scene One: Assembly

Edwin, an editor, enters with an enormous leap (two inches), dances to his desk and assembles a large piece of yellow cardboard, some sticky tape, scissors, coloured paper, photocopied words, a newspaper masthead and some Prit. He juggles with these and produces a Valentine's card. We were all expecting a ransom demand.

Scene Two: Finance

Receptionist Harriet Lang enters and dances her concern for the town's traffic problems. She collects money from the editor and skips to a nearby florist's to buy a bouquet.

Scene Three: Appointment

Edwin mime-dances a long telephone call to the Mayor and agrees to meet her at 4pm – not exactly the witching hour, but pretty close to teatime. Harriet returns with the flowers.

Scene Four: Epistle

Chief reporter Beeno, the human elephant, lumbers on and mimes writing a message on the inside of the card. Pages and pages of district council documents are pinned to his jumper.

Scene Five: Frenzy

Edwin assembles his troops. Harriet dances in with the flowers and out again, Beeno dons an anorak and does the dance of the uncomfortable reporter and Roly Hill the chief photographer enters and bobs about in a puzzled frenzy.

Scene Six: Embarrassment

Mrs Edwin, wife of Edwin, appears unexpectedly to find her husband holding a bouquet of flowers and a Valentine Card. Edwin bobs to and fro in the Dance of the Embarrassed Editor. He mimes 'These are not for you, but they are for the Mayor and are a gift from the paper rather than from me.' Beeno and Roly help unknot his legs after the tricky exposition.

Scene Seven: Journey

In a complex piece of choreography, Edwin, Beeno and Roly mimic travelling the half mile to the Town Hall by car and taking longer to locate a parking space than it would have taken them to walk to the building backwards.

Scene Eight: Presentation

Edwin presents the card and flowers to the Mayor, who does a quick gavotte of delight.

Scene Nine: Snaps

Roly photographs Mayor while Edwin photographs Roly photographing Mayor. Beeno attempts to hide his abashment by secreting himself behind the curtains of the Mayor's Parlour and pretending to be a coat tree.

Scene Ten: Tour

Edwin is given a guided waltz through the town museum by the curator where he spends several minutes attempting to locate the mouse in a Cuneo railway painting.

Scene Eleven: Return

The team return to the office and perform a prance of joy at a job well done.

Scene Twelve: Finale

The entire staff of the paper can-can across the stage with their copies of the February 14 issue of the paper held out in front of them. On the front page there is a picture of the Mayor with her bouquet and card. There is much rejoicing.

I might add that, despite the behind-the-scenes activities viewed here by a jaundiced journo, the Mayor was delighted and touched by the unexpected gesture and it made a really nice front page picture. So it was all worthwhile just for that.

She said afterwards: "Did he make the card himself? Oh, that was sweet."

Or, as the more cynical of us added, "personal... yet so *inexpensive*."

Sadly, that wasn't the end of a wheeze most of us in the news room hoped had gone away.

When the whole ghastly event came round again Edwin, flushed with the success of the previous encounter, decided the paper should this time present Valentine cards to a selected nurse at each of two hospitals in the circulation area.

On this occasion reporting staff begged him to BUY two cheap Valentine cards rather than embarrass everyone by making them himself, whilst clearly under the influence of the do-it-at-home ethos of *Blue Peter*. Thankfully he decided not to pack his desk with toilet roll tubes and "sticky-back plastic" and acceded to the desperate request.

However, he then decided to photocopy the paper's masthead twice, cut them out and strip them diagonally across the bottom of the two cards, drawing a thick felt pen border around each to highlight the paper's name. There was a small floral posy to go with each card (a forward-thinking precaution in case one of the recipients should die at the last minute, presumably).

Chief photographer Roly talked the editor into making the presentations personally, mainly because the redoubtable lens man, who lived near one of the hospitals, couldn't bring himself to be laughed across the ward for such a makeshift offering on his own. They were, like the Mayor's presentation the previous year, scheduled for front page coverage with the pictures being taken before Valentine's Day so their appearance could coincide with the paper's publication day, just after the event. The day chosen for the snaps was, coincidentally but appropriately enough, Comic Relief day.

Things did not begin well with the editor going off sick just before big event. He delegated his deputy Tom to make the card presentation at one hospital and Roly (severely reluctantly) to perform the second one solo. Tom was not pleased but highly embarrassed, a condition accompanied by quite a bit of muttering that was less than supportive of the whole venture.

Tom was even more narked when he discovered that his chosen hospital had picked THREE nurses for the special valentine, but he only had the one card. From his sick bed Edwin approved the purchase of three single roses to cover the clanger. When Tom arrived at the hospital he and the deputy photographer were firstly mistaken for visitors coming to see a patient, and then they got the sex of the hospital secretary wrong, asking for a Mr instead of a Mrs. But eventually they found themselves in a side room ready to make the presentations.

One of the nurses hadn't turned up because she thought, being Comic Relief day, that it was all a joke, though she was eventually rounded up. The next recipient was a lady of more advanced years who had already passed the point of anticipating a valentine from anyone, and the third – wait for it – was not a woman.

As Tom related it afterwards, indignantly: "I had to give this rose to a *man*!"

Pictures appeared as scheduled: happy nurses holding roses in one edition and a single nurse with her card in the other. Roly said nothing about his encounter, though he did adopt a cold stare and allowed a deep sigh to cut through his tightly-sealed lips.

Dictates
Switched On... and Off

One morning, the following memorandum landed on all our desks from the company's "Technical Director." We were so grateful for its helpful guidance.

"WHAT?!"
(Switch-bored operator)

NEW SWITCHBOARD INSTALLATION

The installation of the new telephone switchboard is now complete and to ensure efficient use of the equipment the following procedures will be effected.

The alarm key will be functional during normal office hours, thus the operator will be aware of the user requiring attention immediately the extension hand-set is lifted.

The operator will answer the extension before switching through to outside lines or extension as requested.

Users will be patient and await reply by the operator. "Buzzing" to attract attention will cause complication at the switchboard and can only result in further delay.

The equipment is new to us and a period of trial is obviously necessary with patience exercised by all staff.

The simple user drill will be as follows:-
1. Lift receiver and wait
2. When answered by the operator saying "switchboard," ask for "line out please" or the internal service required
3. When given the line, dial in the normal manner

NOTE: THE TELEPHONE SERVICE IS VERY EXPENSIVE - USE IT AS ECONOMICALLY AS POSSIBLE.

Taking a Break, or Braking a Taking

An internal memorandum which dropped on desks started off promisingly (or ominously, depending on your view of the company you work for) with the line *We all enjoy taking holidays and they are usually fun and well deserved.* Good so far, yet you could feel the grey clouds sneaking up over the skyline.

It went downhill from there, describing the "serious bottlenecks" caused by people taking their holidays during the actual holiday period which, as we all know, is a very narrow window in the UK weather-wise.

The memo did not mention – and we have all been there – that if you employ sufficient staff in the first place you have more-or-less enough bodies to cover absences for holidays (and sickness). Still, the boffins at the top had cracked it!

For the holiday period January to December the company proposes to introduce

a new system for booking holiday entitlement which will work as follows:

One weeks annual holiday to be taken between January 1st and March 31st

Three weeks annual holiday to be taken between April 1st and October 31st

Remaining week to be taken as odd days
Holidays preferably not to be taken in November and December
There is no provision for leave to be carried forward to future
years.

Ah, such fun and so well deserved...

Subordinate

I took over a paper's weekly shipping column for a time, which incorporated lists of ship movements to and from the port, which we got from the coastguards, and features on interesting vessels in dock that week.

For one of these pieces I got to go aboard an Oberon Class submarine, HMS Ocelot. I interviewed her Captain, met some of the crew (five of whom were studying for 'O' levels) and took the tour, squeezing down narrow corridors, swinging legs-first through watertight hatches and peering into tiny cubicles – one of which was smaller than a very modest kitchen and turned out to be both living and sleeping accommodation for the boat's seven officers.

After the article appeared, my editor received a brusque memo from one of the company's editorial directors, a man who was rarely seen and when spotted was always driving a conspicuous and expensive sports car. His finger clearly on the pulse, he called for the shipping column to be "bucked up" as it was clear that the submarine article had been written from a Press release. As someone who had spent a windy Saturday morning in the shipyard to get the piece, I was more than a little miffed.

He also took umbrage at the paper's periodic use of contractions of Christian names accusing reporters of being too "matey." He felt it was over-familiar and possibly embarrassing to the person involved. And he may have had a point, though he seemingly ignored the possibility that the people involved may have preferred and sanctioned the chosen soubriquet. He went on to say that before long we would be referring to company heads as "Ginger" or "Sid" and set out a plan for how to address one of them, namely the Captain of the local shipyard: rather than being referred to as "Gerry" he should be "Captain H. G. Southwood and, later in the same report, Captain Southwood." I would have used "Capt Gerald..." rather than *Gerry*, which was rather discourteous for someone of local standing and professional competence. But I have always baulked at the buttoned-up Victorian idea that everyone should be designated by their initials. There's nothing wrong with a good forename.

Censored

From time to time over the years and at several newspapers I drew gently satirical farewell cards for some departing staff. For example, a chum of mine used to work for the circulation department of a Cornish newspaper and was renowned for regularly denting his company van when on assignment. So when he moved on I drew an outline map of Cornwall with cartoons of his van littered around the county in various states of mechanical distress. These farewell cards would drift around the staff and those who wanted to would sign them with their own good will messages.

However, on one occasion I clearly went too far with the satire. One staffer had unfortunately had a minor heart attack at his desk and had to be carted away by ambulance. He turned out to be fine, but shortly after the incident he decided to chuck in the towel and resign. I drew my customary card – though this time with a little more bite than usual, with a bubble caption based on the chap's long-standing complaints about his tiny office and all its associated health travails – and off it went around the offices. But it never came back and, instead, a large floral card from Woolworths began circulating. I asked where my card had gone and was told "We've lost it." I sensed that the word "lost" has taken on the dimensions of "deliberately dumped it, you company-disloyal lout!"

Maybe, charitably, they were concerned the wording might upset the recipient. But I doubt it. More likely that the truth stung. So I re-drew a better and even more sarcastic (and accurate) version of the card and its sentiments and gave it to the chap myself, as my own personal card to him. He was not upset, but laughed generously.

"How could I forget? Ah, well, there was the time that I worked in a cupboard in an old shed and the toilets used to leak through on to the carpet and the yobs in the next-door correction centre used to ride round and round on motorbikes outside making a hell of a din and the window had to be replaced because it was rotting through and then there was all that fuss about the health department and the next thing my head hit the desk and I ended up in a nurse's arms..."

I had forgotten I did not work for satirical masters *Private Eye* and that there were company managers who did not take kindly to suggestions that their care of employees was rather less than beneficent. Just as well they didn't see the replacement lines above, and their footnote...

"...and then they actually lost my card at HQ – a multi-million pound operation like this (well, £250 a year and still counting toilet rolls) can't even hold on to a bit of cardboard!"

Part 7

People

Memorable people
Letters of thanks
More tales from the lens
Poetic, just as
More trainee fun
Making a living

Memorable People

You meet a lot of diverse people in this job...

Shop girl

A little girl of twelve or thirteen and her mother were ushered into the newsroom one afternoon by the receptionist who said they had a tale to tell and I sat them down next to my desk. With the office being open plan, everyone could overhear everyone else, but I had nowhere private to take clients at that time. So I spoke quietly to them both, in the hope that they would take my lead.

The mother, clearly very angry about the situation she wanted to describe, explained that her daughter has been unfairly accused of stealing from their local village shop and that the shop owners had put a sign on the shop door barring three named teenagers from entering the premises, one of them being her daughter. She felt this was wrong and possibly libelous and put her entirely innocent daughter in a bad light. Could I please write a story about this unjustified slur?

I turned to the girl, who was a pretty normal looking youngster and an unlikely candidate for the ranks of violent hoodie or seasoned criminal, such as the Great Train Robbery brigade. She explained that it had all happened after she and her two friends were in the shop together after school one day and the other two had been carrying out some light pilfering.

"Did *you* take anything?" I asked. The girl said no, and it was clear she wasn't lying.

"Well, have you *ever* stolen anything from that shop?" I asked.

I could hear my deputy, who had clearly been listening in, take a sharp intake of breath in the other corner.

"Oh, *yes*," said the girl unexpectedly and with such candour and conviction that it brooked no dissent. Her mother looked stunned, then daggers at her daughter.

"Well, I congratulate you on your honesty, but I'm afraid there's not much I can do about this now," I told her.

I did suggest to the mother that while the shop owners had every right to decide who they would or would not invite into their property, she could look at the legal aspect of their naming their daughter disadvantageously on a public sign – though the notice made no specific accusations and was merely suggestive of wrong-doing. But I think for the mother that was the end of the matter.

When they had left my colleague turned to me: "I would never have asked her *that*!" he said, taken aback.

"Surely that was the one question that should be asked," I replied.

I never heard any more about it. But I hope the little girl allowed the honest part of her nature to take over from the impish, unlawful dares of her peers.

Life's a gas(sing)

A periodic arts correspondent for one of the papers I served was a passionate consumer of garlic. Unfortunately, it was so strong that you could literally smell him coming – when he was outside the building – and holding a conversation with him at close range became torture as you gagged for breath in the sour and stifling cloud that wafted around you accompanying his energetic chatter.

He was especially keen on cornering the editor in his office, and the editor had a tiny enough room to start off with without having all the oxygen sucked out of it in one intense visit. It became such a regular event that the editor begged us to tell the gentleman (who I will kindly, if a little floridly, refer to as Mr Bardlefardle) that he was OUT whenever the dratted fellow called. This was not easy, as garlic's top advocate tended to wander into the newsroom of his own accord without being announced.

After the editor's latest entreaty for us to please keep the chap away to prevent him choking to death, I presented my boss with the solution to his problem. But I don't think he ever adopted it...

Yes, Mr Bardlefardle...?

In dusky memory

One of the paper's village correspondents was quite elderly, thin, rather cadaverous-looking, and prone to creative flights of fancy in his reports. We'll call him Peter Scone.

His *piece de résistance* came one morning when he submitted a funeral report on a popular local farmer. In an attempt to add some colour and a genuine sense of loss into his piece, he poignantly wrote: *His final words were "what a wonderful sunset."*

To a younger reporter like me, and an even younger and boisterous trainee at the adjoining desk, this was a description too far. We asked ourselves: How did our correspondent know this? Was he standing behind the late farmer, waiting for him to cast off the mortal coil, pencil at the ready? (Of course, he was probably told this by a family member who was there at the time).

Anyway, this led to a slightly unkind cartoon.

Happy farmer watches his last sunset while the Spectral Scone waits behind, notebook poised for his final utterances...

Puzzle

I came up with this unkind doodle (*overleaf*) one day in a moment of reckless inactivity. I shall say no more, being anxious not to be incarcerated for ill-advised royal flippancy.

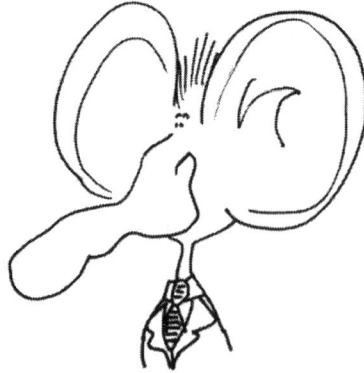

This week's Puzzle Personality (answers on a postcard)

A stunning place to be

A newcomer to the advertising department decided to throw open wide her window, dear (a Benny Hill reference), on a bright, sunny morning. This was partly to welcome a fresh new day and partly to allow some unpolluted air to disperse some of the prevailing fug of her manager's cigar smoke.

There was a sudden *bonk* and a passing customer outside was rendered temporarily senseless as the frame wacked her on the head. Fortunately, she recovered swiftly enough but did her business even more quickly before wandering off, ensuring she kept several feet away from the side of the building until she was clear of it.

Op it!

When one of the reporting team went into hospital for a minor op, she returned to a 'welcome back' card with the following drawing and speech bubble "*I only went in for removal of a mole...*" plus the line "*While you were away we donated your body to science. The men will be in to pick it up at ten.*"

Who? (Not an owl)

Whenever anyone left the newspaper fold, someone would always come around brandishing a farewell card to sign and (often) an envelope for a cash donation to a farewell gift.

On one occasion a chap called Len was leaving the advertising staff. In this case he had not been there very long and worked from a district office so none of the editorial team had any idea who he was.

Sam (*perusing card*): "*We will miss you*??? I've never met him!"

Adrian: "I don't know who he is either."

Tom: "He's the one who sells space for the properties pages out of the branch office. The ex-policeman."

Sam (*signing card, aloud*): "Goodbye, Len, whoever you are..."

Whitney: "It's been nice not knowing you."

Copy on Wheels

A motorcycle courier was employed by one of my newspapers to carry various communications, letters, adverts and news copy between head office and the sub-offices.

He arrived early one morning in his combat jacket and helmet and was standing around in the news room looking uncomfortable (like most of the staff tended to do) when Editor Edwin emerges from his office and goes into his "Hold on a minute... take a seat... would you like a cup of coffee?" routine. This made the lanky lad look even more anxious. He shuffled uneasily, clutching the hot chocolate he had requested, and responded: "I'm going out to check my oil."

He does that and returns a few minutes later, hovers about and Edwin repeats, more pressingly: "DO have a seat." The courier still declines. Enter reporter Adrian, returning from the front office. He spies the courier. "Would you like a seat?" he asks.

The guy couldn't get out of the place quickly enough.

One day a new advertising assistant, unfamiliar with staff, popped her head around the news room door and asked: "Who is Tom Sears?"

Deputy editor Tom raises his head: "Me."

Ad lass: "Your son is outside to see you."

Tom (*standing*): "Right."

Ad lass (*to much mirth*): "We thought it was the courier."

Feted

One of my colleagues regularly insisted on using the phrase "a damp squid" in her stories about any matter or event that has failed to come up to expectation; something that doesn't *go off* according to plan. A squid that's damp would just be a normal occurrence within its own environment, of course.

This is understandable as it is apparently the most frequent of misquotes by Brits, heading a top ten including on *tender* hooks (instead of *tenter*), one *foul* swoop (instead of *fell*) and all that *glitters* is not gold (instead of *glisters*). And there's the perennial favourite *cold slaw*. All up there with the trainee who referred to an historic church's *rude* screen.

We've all been there in moments of distraction but, once, her squiddy phrase actually appeared in a front page story, which is always a mite embarrassing as it's hard to miss in that location and journalists are supposed to be guardians of accuracy. (*Hah!* I hear you cry, cynically).

This particular aquatic bloomer was highlighted in a mock story on the reporter's farewell card when she moved on to pastures new. As she was a diver in her leisure time, the tale told of her search for "the illusive damp squid," with the brilliant headline (top marks to the sub!) *Aegean snorkel begins Operation Wet Cephalopod*.

However, her best misconception in this area was when she filed a report about a local Summer *Bizarre*. This time the sub struck back and she found the following handwritten comment on her corrected story: "Must have been a *fete* worse than death..."

A puff too far

One female reporter, in her twenties, took to smoking a pipe. Though there is no reason why a woman should not smoke a pipe, except for the common sense health reasons that apply to us all, it seemed a bit odd back in the early 1970s, a time when women usually did not indulge. As I recall it, it was nothing modest, of meerschaum proportions, and looked a mite ridiculous – more like a bubble pipe, as my sketch recorded – especially for a slim, long-haired young lass noted for wearing flowing, flowery dresses and cascading beads rather than professorial tweeds. I seem to recall the fad didn't last long.

The only time I tried a pipe, I stuffed it full of Condor, lit up, took a generous drag, turned to speak to a colleague, choked as the noxious fumes hit my lungs, turned green, began coughing frantically and came the second-nearest to passing out that I have ever experienced (the first being after downing half a pint of beer shandy in a pub whilst badly sunburned: I saw a dark corridor closing in and saved myself from pirouetting to the floor by struggling outside and gasping in as much fresh air as I could inhale). Needless to say, the pipe became a family heirloom in the bottom of a bottom drawer.

Crunch time

The editor was awaiting his new company car, which had been on order for weeks, and was getting quite restless about it. Finally one morning his new Peugeot was delivered and carefully parked in the company car park, just inside the entrance: the perfect place, in fact, for a large lorry delivering newsprint rolls to plunge into it just a few hours later. To his distress the editor then saw his long-awaited new company car being towed back to the garage, badly dented, before he'd even had a chance to sit in it, let alone drive it home.

"Fluttering" MP

A few decades ago, the local Member of Parliament made a trip behind the Iron Curtain, as part of some trade delegation as far as I recall. Naturally, our paper reported this unexpected journey and I thought I would illustrate the text with a couple of cartoons parodying the unusual escapade.

So I dashed off the drawings and presented them to the sub-editor the next morning with a degree of anticipation and sadly misplaced confidence. He cast a casual eye over them both but didn't seem to get either of the jokes.

The first cartoon showed the returned politician expressing what he had learned from his foreign jaunt by Cossack-dancing on a table at a Parliamentary select committee. The second showed him landing at a foreign airport and being welcomed by a contingent of enthusiastic, placard-waving Wombles.

"What's this all about?" the sub asked.

"The trip by the MP."

"Yes, yes."

"Well, you know, Uncle *Bulgaria*," I said.

The sub gave me a sympathetic but slightly pained glance.

"He's been to *Czechoslovakia*," was all he needed to say.

And, as he hadn't been to Russia either, it was an odds-on certainty that cossack dancing might not have been all that popular in occupied Czechoslovakia. I could have used the arguement that I was adopting a background touch of droll political satire about an MP thinking that the traditional dance of a country was one favoured by its oppressors. But I wasn't.

Anyway, the airport sketch (which I'm still fond of) shows the MP disembarking and an aide asking "Do you think someone is pulling our leg, Sir?" Oh, if only it had been so.

"I see that our Member For has been behind the Iron Curtain again..."

This particular MP was very fond of a flutter – and I don't mean dressing up as a bat. One of his passions was fruit machines.

I went to interview him around the same time as his trip, on a subject long since forgotten, and walked into the men's bar of the area's Constitutional Club one lunchtime – probably not a good moment – to find him positioned at the one-arm bandit, its one arm firmly in his right hand. I then spent the entire duration of the interview standing next to him asking the pertinent questions and writing down his distracted answers while he dropped coin after coin into the hungry gambling slot, pumping the handle like an apprentice boxer.

Goodness, it's Godiva!

What was becoming known as the West Country's favourite woofer-spotting village fair came round again and for the second time it featured a Lady Godiva. The paper sent elderly freelance photographer Dabney Winters to do the honours – he of the less-than-convincing lensmanship. Naturally, the pictures were unusable, but then Dabney was hardly going to suddenly develop a *Penthouse*-style photographic technique over one Saturday afternoon in a village field. AND he'd not got a single villager in the frame. Thankfully we were able to find some alternative shots from elsewhere that were perfectly acceptable.

The other down side was that the body-stockinged and bewigged lady who was repeating her performance from the previous year had gained quite of bit of weight in the intervening months and looked, as chief reporter Beeno unkindly remarked to his editor, "not unlike a whale on a horse."

This was rather uncalled for, as the former model was a delightful and popular lass and did much for the good spirits of the village in question and its coffers. Even so, the horse did look like it was under a bit of pressure.

The year before, and the first time the Godiva ride-through was staged, the pictures were better and the writing pretty upbeat. There were lots of pictures of local people and the Lady herself smiling and laughing on what was clearly a cheerful, sunny day. The paper carried a couple of separate pieces with pictures, though the danger of carrying text and pictures of a "naked" woman in a "family" newspaper is that the power to inadvertently offend is always lurking – even if she is clad in a body stocking.

So when Sam opened the paper on publication day and surveyed his subbing work on the text he was visibly relieved that he had amended the line in the caption of a picture showing a local policeman with Lady Godiva on his lap: it had originally read that the PC "gave her a friendly lap," within which Sam had detected cunnilingial overtones. However, someone else, probably the deputy editor, had changed Sam's alteration to "gave a friendly seat," which Sam did not appreciate as an alternative, possibly because of some implied pedication. But he almost burst a blood vessel when he saw Tom's headline on the main story, which read: *I'd like to come again says Godiva.*

Meanwhile, the organiser said the event went without incident, except for some hapless amateur photographer who was thumped by his wife for trying to get a candid snap of the bubbling beauty.

Making a fist of it

One morning I was called to the office reception area to find an unlikely duo. One was a Goliath of a man, muscular and dressed casually, and he was accompanied by a much slighter gentleman, dressed in a smart suit. At first glance, and not unkindly, they looked like a circus strongman and his ringmaster. The truth wasn't far removed from this.

The former was a bare-knuckle boxer and the latter, with his thin moustache and bow tie, reminded me of a more diminutive version of the friendly cockney spiv Walker from the TV series *Dad's Army*. He introduced the pair of them and thereafter referred to me as "Sir" throughout the interview, in a slightly reverential rather than a sarcastic way, which was gratifying.

The point of the visit was that the boxer and his "manager" wanted some publicity for a bare knuckle boxing bout that was due to take place in a few days time. He told me that such money-making tournaments were currently illegal, which was why it was being staged on a boat in the harbour rather than on land.

I noted the details, wrote the story and the fight took place as scheduled, though I understand that police took to boats in an attempt to foreshorten the event and scold those attending it.

I found the "manager" and his charge, who described themselves as genuine Romany gipsies, to be both polite and charming. The boxer himself was indeed a gentle giant and, though I would not have fancied being on the wrong end of his massive iron-like fists, I found my twenty minutes chatting to him and his colleague most engaging and non-threatening, belying their first appearance.

Over the years I have engaged with all sorts of people from all walks of life, from occasional Lords of the Manor (whose jolly comportment suggested they had been dropped on their heads when young) to "roughies" on council estates (who looked like they could slam you through a plaster wall with a flick of the wrist).

I've even been backed up against the stippling in the waiting room of a Magistrate's Court by a young black chap concerned that if I published his case (a very minor infringement) he might lose his job and reputation, especially because of his skin shading. It was not, as it appeared at the outset, a deliberate attempt to intimidate, but a simple case of a different body language where some races stand closer to each other than others, as described by Desmond Morris in his fascinating 1977 book *Manwatching*.

From these kind of situations you learn not to coldly condemn a person purely on the basis of their race, religion, colour, social status, hobbies, eccentricities, partners, skills or physical appearance. We need a lot more positive abandonment of pre-judgement these days for us to survive prejudice and to make the world a more harmonious place. Of course, some people will still be insufferable swine whatever you do.

Letters of thanks

It's always nice to receive letters of thanks from readers. Actually, it's a great honour coupled with a delight to know that you've done something to brighten someone's day from just doing your job.

I'm fortunate to have received several kind compliments during my newspaper career, including one from the Local Government Ombudsman of the day who both commended me for a sterling piece but also admitted that errors in the figures published were entirely his own, as he'd not been given the correct brief at the time.

But my favourite of all of them was a handwritten letter from an 85-year-old retired Cornish miner way back in the early 1970s, when I was still new to journalism.

I had come across the remains of an old mine under a railway viaduct in the village of Ponsanooth and began doing a bit of digging – not literally, though I did visit the site, recklessly clambering around its overgrown slopes oblivious of the possibility that I might suddenly disturb an old shaft and vanish from view, and probably this life.

The village, between Penryn and Redruth, already had some historic industrial prominence through the activities of flour, gunpowder and paper mills on the nearby River Kennall in the 19th century. My focus, which I found was the Magdalene Mine, produced black tin (cassiterite), a raw ore needing several purging processes before becoming saleable – pretty much the opposite of the refined metallic "white tin" that appears after smelting. The mine operated on and off between the mid 16th century and the 1930s.

After the feature appeared I had a call from probably the last surviving miner to work the Magdalene's shafts and adits. He was called Joe and I arranged to meet him and write a follow-up piece, all about him. He was a charming, heavy-set yet graceful man, with a lovely twinkle in his eye and, over tea in china cups, he told me of his days underground and on the surface, labouring 50ft below the clattering wheels of the steam trains trundling across the Brunel-designed viaduct. Staff photographer Peter Chesworth took a snap of him wearing a Cornish tartan flat cap, round-lensed spectacles, a knitted jumper and his generous smile, and a couple of weeks later the story appeared. It began:

Joe B--- is a miner. Although he is 85 and long since retired from the mines, a glint still catches his eye when anybody mentions the Magdalene

Mine tin deposits at Ponsanooth. He worked there for ten years and that
certain something that makes a miner is still in his blood...

After publication, we sent Joe some gratis copies of his picture and within days the letter arrived. I still have it, and treasure it. He was delighted by the snaps and, dubbing the lens man "a Master Photographer," added that "while the Packet has such fine reporters and photographers the Packet is bound to get better every year. I have been reading the Packet for years now and enjoy it very much. Keep up the good work for it is very interesting for us all. All the best and good luck to you both."

A heartfelt nod that was worth my pay cheque (and more) that week.

Footnote for the fastidious. In Cornish, Ponsanooth means "bridge at the stream" and its most famous son was amateur botanist Frederick Hamilton Davey (1868-1915) who wrote the renowned *Flora of Cornwall*; he began work in the village powder mills at 11 and is buried in the local Wesleyan cemetery.

More Tales From the Lens

Parsimonious Company opts for nice, traditional freelance photographer (i.e. cheap)

Strawberry Runner

For a while the news room employed an elderly freelance photographer to carry out assignments when the staffers weren't available. He was frankly a terrible photographer, but he was a really nice, good-humoured and accommodating chap who would do anything, any time for anyone and (the important issue here) charged next to nothing for his services. We'll call him Dabney Winters.

As examples of his renowned work, on one occasion he photographed a group of dancers from the back, so that none of their faces could be seen; on another he took a snap of a swimming gala from the far end of the pool. A vast expanse of empty water lay between his lens and the one hundred or so contestants clustered at the Deep End away in the far, far distance. None of their faces were recognisable, and there were just two tiny heads in the water. If we had tried to blow the image up to make the faces visible the fuzzy image would have needed to be cropped and spread over two pages.

Well, dear old Dabney was sent to cover the annual bed race organised by a local Rotary Club. He subsequently submitted a selection of pictures which, quite frankly, were not up to par. In fact, the best thing to do with them would have been to pack them under the wonky leg of an editorial desk.

The worst was the one of the "Strawberry Buggy." For a start it was incredibly blurry. Its name was a puzzle too, as it looked like an ordinary and rather makeshift wooden go kart – the sort you used to knock together as kids to ride down that dodgy hill close to your house until you finally crash it and gain your first important battle scars. Anyway.

Reporter Beeno said to Tom the sub: "You can't use that. It's all out of focus."

Tom sighed. "I've got to use it – they're the winners," he replied, reading Dabney's caption handwritten in biro on the back of the print. Then he added: "It won't look so bad if I use it small."

Beeno said he was not convinced. He was even less convinced when he saw the resulting caption, a sub's desperate attempt to explain the out-of-focus shot...

So fast they're just a blur: the winners of the bed race – Strawberry Buggy.

The morning that the piece appeared (incorporating two other slightly better pictures and some general blurb), the paper got a phone call from a local youth club leader whose boys' team we claimed had come second, as per Dabney's caption. In fact, they came first.

"Oh," said Beeno. "Then the Strawberry Buggy came second."

"No," said the youth leader. "I don't know where they came in; second was..." and he gave Beeno the name of a local garage.

When Beeno explained that the paper had only been using the photographer's captions, the youth club leader said: "Yes, well, Strawberry Buggy might have come IN first, but it certainly wasn't the winner because the race had a staggered start."

The moral of this story: never rely on photographers' captions and always check results of events with the organisers. It is true that the organisers don't always get it right either, but at least you have done your bit for the cause of accuracy and at the same time absolved the paper of responsibility for any errors.

(Not) hiding the unpleasant truth

Regarding complaints, one paper – rather bravely for a small, local weekly – once carried a front page photograph of the aftermath of a very public suicide. It didn't show the victim, who had jumped from the top floor of a local multi-storey car park, but included the area where it had happened, an ambulance, police, etcetera, along with the full story.

One reader complained that she had been so shocked by this that she turned the paper face down so that "the children couldn't see it," only to be confronted with a back page photograph of a low-loader packed with dead moorland sheep that had been savaged by dogs. She protested: "I had to take the outer pages off and throw them away!"

In the end, you have to make certain decisions about how you cover local news balanced against its effects on readers. In the end I think the right decision was made to print the two items, though the distressed reader would disagree. A complaint was even lodged with the Press Complaints Commission on grounds of taste but was not upheld.

A freelance photographer not customarily noted for putting names on photo captions sent in two pictures of prize-giving ceremonies at a local school. One photograph showed eight boys with a caption containing nine names; the other showed 13 girls with 12 names.

A dour, humourless girl joined the photographic department for a two week work experience stint.

Reporter (*commenting to Chief Photographer on the character of his new charge*): "I thought YOU were a miserable bugger."

Chief Photographer: "I can't get her to smile. I can't even get her to swear."

Trainee: "Well, she'll be no good at that job, then."

When the company's expenses rates increased one of the photographers was the first to have his claim cut, to offset the improvements. He was told by his editor: "There is no need to charge for a lunch time job if you can take your lunch early to overcome it."

Photographer Cary Grantham is on a photo assignment when the office camera breaks down (again). Fortunately he has a spare and is able to complete the job. When he gets back to the office he takes the camera to Edwin (for the umpteenth time) and re-explains their condition and that they aren't worth repairing. Edwin disagrees and asks Cary if he will use one of his own cameras until the company ones are fixed. Cary says no, he's not bringing in his personal equipment for company use, to which Edwin says, "Well, I'd better bring mine in then." And does...

The first closed cycle race in the area was staged in the town centre one bright summer evening. The main street was closed off, and the cyclists raced for an hour on a circular course. Photographer Cary Grantham was told to take his pictures standing on a well-sited lorry with a "stage" opening out from the side. As he mounted the steps, the rival evening paper's photographer appeared round the corner and said magnanimously: "Here, this is our van – fuck off." It turned out that they had loaned their own company van, with its name plastered everywhere, to the organisers. Cary went back and stood in the street.

Edwin had promised a particular school that we would take a photograph of their carnival float entry which was travelling around the various carnivals in the area; we would do it at their next outing as we'd missed snapping them at three carnivals already.

Eventually Edwin told both photographers: "The next carnival you do, get a picture of that school float. It will be more than my life's worth if you don't."

To which chief photographer Roly Hill smiled and murmured: "More than his life's worth, eh? I'll make a point of missing it!"

Edwin brought in a film to process of the dedication of a new bench by some primary school children. Roly noted ulcerously that almost every picture showed about a dozen kids sitting on the garden seat, so that the seat was totally obscured. He was not at impressed by this, and told Edwin. Edwin told him to produce a print of the children on the seat.

Roly: "But you can't see the seat. I thought they were supposed to be dedicating it."

Edwin (*not to be sidetracked*): "Well, if they are sitting on it they are dedicating it."

There were many occasions when reporters and subs were left chewing the corners of their desks (not really; bad for the molars) whilst waiting for photographers to produce the prints of their assignments. On one occasion these often unnecessary delays came home to roost (to mix metaphors), more of less.

Chief photographer Roly (*pontificating on a local quick-print photo processors*): "This lot can do it while you wait – in an hour."

Beeno (*surprised, as this was in the Eighties and he had been thinking the quickest turn-around would be overnight*): "An hour?"

Roly: "Yea. Of course. It doesn't take any time to develop a film. It's five minutes to dip, nine minutes to print and wash and another five to dry..."

Beeno: "Then three days to get it from Photographic to the News Room."

Roly (*long pause; finally a grin*): "Well, there's the admin work..."

Some photographic paper arrived in Editorial. It was securely wrapped in a large parcel marked *Open only in darkroom conditions*. Edwin grabbed it and headed for Photographic. The following exchange followed.

Edwin (*placing parcel next to chief photographer Roly Hill*): "Roly, this is for you, I think."

Roly (*taking parcel, glancing at it and moving it to one side before continuing with what he's doing*): "Yes."

Edwin (*suspiciously*): "Well, er, it's very large."

Roly: "It's large photographic paper."

Edwin (*not to be put off, as he is trying to make a point about company costs without actually mentioning them*): "Well, why is it so BIG?"

Roly: "Because you can't get 20x15 paper in an 8 x 6 box, Edwin."

Roly's assistant Cary Grantham (*piping up*): "Unless you fold it."

End of discussion.

Poetic, Just As

There are times when readers become quite creative when contacting their local papers – and they often get creative replies too. Here's one instance of a delightful letter sent to the *Mid-Devon Advertiser* some years ago, and the response from the news room, proving that we like to help when we can, and I hope we did. The letter read:

> There was a young girl
> Let's call her a fan
> Of Eddie Izzard
> That humorous man.
> He featured in Taunton
> On Monday last week
> And he tickled her fancy
> With his wit and his cheek.
> When she sat down to breakfast
> The very next day
> With the Mid-Devon paper
> Dated the tenth of May
> There was a picture
> Of Eddie and crew
> So, please send a photo
> Two copies will do

The reply (which has been amended to protect the name and address of the source of the snap by the italic changes) read:

> You sent us a poem (did it take you hours?)
> About Eddie Izzard and his comic powers
> His fun and his genius that really towers
> But the snapshot you're seeking is not one of ours!
> Still, do not start weeping or gnashing your gums
> For I have an answer, so cross both your thumbs.
> It came from the Brewhouse in Taunton to me
> From their duo who deal with their publicity
> The actual source is *Fran Morton* I see
> At *22 Wilson Road, London,* whose fee
> I am unaware of, why not pick up a pen
> And write to her (*dot-dot dot-dot*) 8NN?

More Trainee Fun

You always did your best to explain to new trainees matters such as house style (that's whether or not the paper allows you to start a sentence with *And*, when to use capital letters, and so on) and how you transform a bare-bones wedding report into a story. Sometimes, we journalists run away with language and obscure what we mean. Hence this little exchange.

Editor Edwin: "Beeno, have you introduced our new trainee Terry to our wedding sequence?"

Chief Beeno: "No. Terry – boy meets girl, girl meets boy; they meet at church..."

OR

Trainee (*typing a wedding report*): "Is 'best man' usually in caps?"

Senior reporter: "No, they're usually in top hats."

QUOTE OF THE WEEK: Trainee Whitney refers to "a flood elevation scheme." (It should have been *alleviation*. I know, you got it).

When one of the advertising girls got hit in the face with a hockey stick during a match and got herself hospitalised, a trainee wrote in her get well card from the staff: *Why didn't you send us a report of the match?*

A new trainee, rewriting a Women's Institute report, referred to one of the members as "Mrs Mesdames."

All Wrapped Up

One trainee was offered a free trial of a new sauna-style weight loss regime – all for the price of some free publicity for a new local business run by local folk. So she set off. When she got there she discovered that the treatment involved stripping naked and having the whole of her body wrapped in bandages – and for a very long time. Rather than transforming into the product of an archaeological dig, she beat a hasty retreat – but not before she'd got the story. Afterwards I recorded the potential consequences had she stayed for the treatment.

Invisible

Whenever a specific day was referred to in a story, such as "on Wednesday," reporters had to place the actual date referred to into their copy, in brackets afterwards, as in "on Wednesday (Mar 4)." Stories were (obviously) written before the next edition was published but did not always appear in that issue, being held over for either available space reasons or if the piece was temporarily supplanted by something more pressing. This allowed the sub to adjust the line to read "last Wednesday" or "next Wednesday," simply "Wednesday," or to leave the day out completely if the piece was postponed for longer.

Sub Sam Trafford looked up one bright morning near to Christmas and, referring to such a practise and to a piece of copy from a new and slightly gullible trainee, said: "Only Terry Mote would write *Boxing Day* then, in brackets, *Dec 26!*"

In fact, young Terry was so innocuous that one evening around 5.30pm Sam was subbing away diligently and was surprised to hear a tiny voice ask "Can I go now?"

Sam looked up to find Terry sitting in a corner of the newsroom and somewhat heartlessly replied: "I didn't realise you were still here."

Mug(gins)

When one of the trainees was named student of the year by the National Council for the Training of Journalists the achievement was rightly reported in his local paper, along with a photograph of a presentation to the clever hack by his editor and sub-editor and the company's vice-chairman.

For his achievement, marking all the hard work and dedication that led up to it, he was given a pewter beer mug and, from the very hand and lips of the vice-chairman, a £1 coin "towards your first pint."

"Thought I might've at least got a pay rise..."

It's a Gas

There was a bit of a scare about Radon gas in the late eighties. The main concern was the amount of these radioactive particles, damaging to the lungs, which might be trapped in properties built on or close to Dartmoor, which has generous deposits of granite, a prime source of the problem.

One trainee was given the Radon assignment and it went on and on and on and on like a tedious after dinner speaker, week after week, becoming more and more frenzied and demanding until the subject finally drifted into local obscurity due to an absence of significant related illness or deaths.

Selected residents were told to seal off flooring and increase ventilation and were also given little Radon-sensitive disks to place in their homes to monitor the situation.

The plucky trainee nearly went mad with the seemingly bottomless and unproductive assignment and its special language (such as learning how to record Radon levels in *becquerels* and *sieverts*) as well as the mostly-unjustified fears of residents that their property prices were about to plummet due to a newly-detected and invisible pestilence.

This was my exaggerated version of the plucky trainee's appearance at the height of the scare, weighted down both with technical data and an ever more hysterical campaign of potential doom.

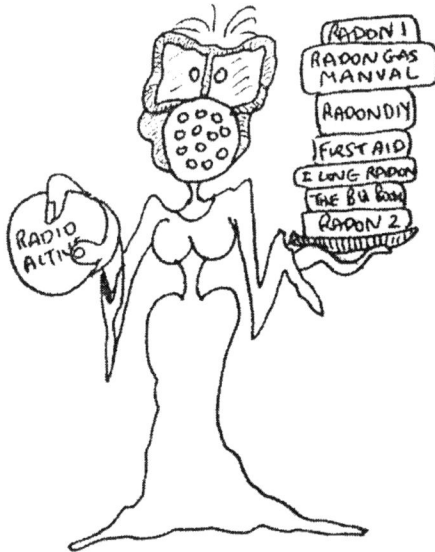

See the noted newshound come
A radon pamphlet in her hand
Through groves of twisted typing stools
In newsrooms mostly barely manned...

Office space

Sometimes district offices are very small, often due to the cost of maintaining a larger unit.

A trainee who had found himself shipped off to one of these far-flung and often lonely outposts, heard that the company was looking for an even smaller place for him to inhabit after receiving an unacceptably high quotation for renovation work on his current squat. At this point I wrote this:

Ace trainee Dan Partridge has saved the company a small fortune by becoming his own office. Dan was so shocked when he learned how much it would cost the company to refurbish his district news room that he set out to solve the problem himself, inventing his own strap-on reporter's desk unit so that he can work standing up in even the smallest space.

"Forget the office. All they need to do now is give me an old wardrobe to work in," he said excitedly.

*Trainee opens mouth too soon, then finds there is
no handle on the inside of his new office-drobe*

[Note: Blacks Bag. "Blacks," as mentioned earlier, was the terms for carbon copies of typed news stories, retained in case the top copy was lost, a term easily misconstrued nowadays.]

Trainee to chief reporter: "Have you just been to the front office?"

Chief: "Yes. Why?"

Trainee (*phone linked to front office pressed to her ear*): "I can hear babies crying."

Chief (*to hoots of office laughter*): "What are you implying by that?"

When trainee Whitney asked her chief reporter how to write a particular news piece, his idiosyncratic instructions included using the non-word "blonk" to indicate the place for the name of a person, location, business or organisation. Within minutes, Whitney had come up with this rather literal response.

The blonk hospital of blonk benefitted from a blonk donation by the blonk branch of the Blonk Inner Wheel. Mrs Blonk, president of the club, presented the £1,500 cheque to the blonk department.

Her chiefy felt a bit of a blonker...

One trainee came up with this sentence: "The council will hold a council meeting just before Christmas dressed in Victorian costume with **candals** instead of electric lighting."

She did not appreciate the constructive criticism lurking in this gently amusing cartoon that I passed to her along with the spelling correction – though I did get a pretty agitated snort of derision, which could have powered a small Meccano steam engine for a good couple of hours...

A BUNCH OF CANDALS.....

Trainee (*putting phone down, in surprise*) "The place is full of bloody Americans!"

Chief Reporter: "Where were you ringing?"

Trainee: "The American Embassy."

Making a Living
(Where many of us end up...)

This was a slightly less frivolous cartoon, describing the close-to-poverty existence that many newspaper trainees suffered if they didn't have caring or wealthy parents to bail them out in their chosen profession.

Financial hardship was one thing that a provincial newspaper trainee reporter could always count on in my day, and it's probably not changed a great deal since, with the exception that there are fewer jobs for novices and fewer titles for them to novice on.

Trainees always (well, mostly) arrived wide-eyed, excited and delighted, and within a few months would be overworked, underpaid, exhausted and living in cheap digs making five-day curries in a battered saucepan and wondering how on earth they were going to afford to keep their old banger of a car on the road. Transport, they were told, was "not a requirement;" but unless you wanted to stay chained to a desk it was often the only way to get out on assignments – as well as back to the family home at the weekend with a pile of washing. Wages were breadline and "expenses" risible.

Yes, there was an argument that the strident life conditions of an apprenticeship prepared you for a tough future in an unsympathetic profession. But mostly that was an excuse for firms to be parsimonious when it came to fiscal reward – what we experienced wordsmiths would call *tight*, or, as one of my colleagues frequently expounded, "tight as a duck's ass – and that's watertight!"

These days, trainees can sometimes find themselves on the streets of their local town giving away copies of their newspaper in some promotional push – a move that is always deemed less expensive, using existing staff at no cost and in their own time, than bringing in private companies to push your product. Sometimes free gifts are given away. I still have one freebie, presented excitedly to me with a paper and a bag of sugary sweets during a local evening paper promotion some while after I had retired from the profession: a pencil inscribed JUNIOR NEWS HOUND.

Still, trainees can be thankful that they no longer have to endure some even more onerous office duties that have largely vanished with time – such as standing outside a parish church collecting the names of mourners at the funeral of a popular civic or professional figure. As one colleague who used to be assigned this thankless task explained: "If you missed just one name there would be complaints from the family, an internal investigation into what went wrong (i.e. how much of a ninny the reporter had been), and a groveling apology in the next issue of the paper."

I was lucky to have missed that dubious task, though for many years I and my colleagues had to type out long and exhaustive lists of family mourners to accompany funeral reports, which often took up columns of tightly-spaced 6pt. And likewise, woe betide you missed an entry or mis-spelled anyone in the blur of handwritten names. Fortunately, this tiresome task was eventually abandoned to give more space to news reports as pagination became tighter through increasingly income-conscious times.

Part 8

A Miscellany of the Skewed

Advertisemental
Bloopers, cock-ups, oddities and odd comments
Cartoons
Cheque up
Out of the mouths of...
You don't have to be mad to work elsewhere too

Advertisemental

Flat spin
A reader tore an advert from the paper
LUXURY FLATS
50 YARDS FROM WATER
From £18,000 – 2-bedroomed
adding his handwritten comment underneath:
Isn't that a bit far to carry the buckets for the luxury baths?

Walking on it?
Spotted on the funny picture board: A photo of two priests standing at the quayside in their long robes and both looking out over the water, with the caption "After you, old chap."

Pets Tour
Advert spotted in the PETS column: *Baby Buggies.*

A Baby Buggy?

This was slightly less embarrassing than an engagement notice placed in the centre of the PETS AND LIVESTOCK column which, in turn, was less excruciating than the joyous announcement in the BIRTHS column that halfway through disastrously changed to *Cremation Friday. Family flowers only...*

Other entries in the Pets column have included

URGENTLY WANTED. Lead, brass, copper, gunmetal, no 2 wire, rolled alloy, iron, batteries...

and

FACELIFT. First-class carpentry, decorating and plumbing...

Jobblessssss
Jobless total soars

Unemployment among people under 25 in Common Market countries has soared by 49 per cent over the past year according to ees dCHRDLBSHRDLSHRD SHR in a draft report by the social affairs department of the EEC commission in Brussels.

Ear Today

I'm not having a pop here at people who need cosmetic help to cover some unfortunate injury, but there are perhaps more sympathetic ways of putting it than in this newspaper piece.

Rubber ears are available to anyone who needs one (or two) on the National Health. They are not usually given to someone before eight years old when the ear stops growing. After the age of eight a patient is entitled to a new rubber ear every year because the old ones become a bit grubby with long use. The rubber is stuck to the head with gum mastic, the special glue used by actors.

"Most people are perfectly satisfied with a rubber ear," said Professor C.

Especially Mr Spock...

Of Men and Mice

Here, the sub-editor has determined that there is a fascinating snippet of hitherto unknown rodentia news in this tale of a local small animal show in fashioning his assertive headline.

MICE DO NOT LIKE TRAINS

"There are some very good entries in the mice classes," said Mr F, "but if course they could be better." He explained that the area's geographical position affected the quality and variety of the entries. Owners in the North of England, where mice-breeding has long been popular, are reluctant to send their mice by train on so long a journey. It means that their little charges are out of their care for about five days and, whoever owns the railways, mice do not care much for train travel.

Which is probably why they're always painted running alongside trains in Cuneo railway pictures rather than relaxing in a seat. Or maybe they're too small to reach up and buy a ticket.

Royal Relation

The Alexandra Hall and the Butter Market were built in 1871 and the hall was intended for a corn exchange but in 1888 the hall was converted into a theatre. It was named after Princess Alexandra, wife of Newton Abbot.

The Play's Our Thing

Extract from a letter from a village pantomime group, attempting to encourage the paper to venture out on a cold night to report on their new production. Sweet thoughts, but a tad effusive for a hardened old hack.

Everyone likes to come to see our plays because they are full of fun and fills the whole world with laughter.
We make people laugh so much that you hear heaven ringing with bells as it starts to open, and then you can hear heaven singing our songs with us.
We try to make the world happy and people forget their worries.

Interesting ads

£499 'C' Morris 1000 Traveller. Blue with Blue trim. Very ccclcllelleleeeeeaaeaannannn fe n for or year. 1965.
German Shepherd Pup Pies, excellent pedigree. £50 each.
MALE (24) seeks doom in central flat. Please phone....
FIVE well-bred Ferrets, only reason for sale, owners leg injuries...

Heavy...

I would have liked to have been at this one...

ROYAL BRITISH LEGION
GRAND DANCE
Braunton Parish Hall
Sat 19th April, 8pm-12
Music by DEEP PURPLE
Bar and Buffet   Ticket £1.50

Motormouthing

After spotting a page of motoring adverts featuring scantily-clad models promoting motor oil, motor bikes and (oddly) a petrol pump, a reporter was complaining to an ad girl that they seemed a bit raunchy for the local paper.

"Oh, that was the motoring guy," she replied, as if that answered everything. "You want to see him about it. I told him about this survey in France that said all men treat their cars just like their women."

"It's just as well I don't do that," replied the reporter, whose wages were barely living standard.

"Why not?" she asked.

"They'd all be covered in rust!" he replied.

Cracked

From my old advertising department days.

Ad Manager: "What are S----'s Pottery like for ads, Ted? Do they play ball?"

Salesman: "Not in the pottery they don't."

Thanks for Nothing

Advert for her own job from disgruntled advertising department employee, leaving for a post with better pay and conditions. Surprisingly, the text was not used.

WANTED
Mature, reliable, hard-working person for
almost full-time vacancy.
Must be prepared to drop everything at a moment's
notice and be always available.

Duties include travelling between offices (usually without expenses), doing more than one person's job at a time, learning a variety of different jobs.

You will get no pension, no holiday pay, no sick pay, no Bank Holiday pay,

no bonus and no training.

Wages will be a basic minimum.

If you are interested, you must be mad.

Apply to *** Newspaper's hit men

at the following address.

Strange Kind of Leisure

Sometimes filling an empty space on a page at the last minute can produce some inadvertent clashes. Probably no more so than in one issue of the paper in the 1980s featuring a special page of boxed advertisements headed LEISURE SCENE – ENTERTAINMENTS, EATING OUT, EVENTS and including boxed adverts in various sizes for a wide range of visitor attractions, plays, films and restaurants.

In the bottom right hand corner of the page was a large promotion for the 50th anniversary screening of Disney's *Snow White and the Seven Dwarfs*, complete with artwork of Snow, her diminutive companions and a couple of pretty song birds – and directly opposite that there was a health authority advert listing FAMILY PLANNING & CYTOLOGY CLINICS and AIDS advice...

Though, perhaps equally unfortunate was a December half page advertising feature from the same year headed GOLLY IT'S CHRISTMAS and including a spot-the-difference competition of a Gollywog opening a large seasonal parcel for which the prize was a 'deluxe recipe' Christmas pudding and a 'super Nurse Golly Doll.'

And if you think I'm going to illustrate that one...

Bloopers, cock-ups, oddities and odd comments

Here's a small collection of "bloopers" – things that newspaper folk such as printers, subs, advertising reps and reporters manage to create so regularly and effortlessly – that I have collected over the years.

He was carried unconscious from an airliner after apparently swallowing a mixture of drink and rugs.

Mrs D, who moved next door to Mrs B about a year ago, told the court that the dogs had made life hell for her. She had complained about them getting into her garden through a solicitor's letter.

On the frequent clash between car users and equestrians, a road safety officer commented: "The problem with some drivers is that they forget that a horse is only human and can be easily frightened."

New technology and advances in installation techniques mean that we can install a comprehensive burglar at very best rates.

A horsewoman was airlifted to hospital after a riding accident on Dartmoor. She is said to be in a stable condition.

SECRETARY
WITH NO TIES FOR SMALL HAULAGE OFFICE

" I'm sorry – you can't have the job..."

He said: "It takes a lot of pleasure away from the sport when you know you are skiing through raw sewage."

A cat burglar has stolen three Jack Russell puppies from an isolated farm near Truro. The officer investigating is PC Jack Russell.

Carnival Queen Miss --- and her attendants won a knobbly knees competition. (Should have been *judged*).

"Most of the employers in the area, particularly those in manufacturing, have extended the Christmas holiday and seem to be away until after the New ear," he said.

During the seventies power crisis this remarkable technological achievement was reported:
Mr J.L.L. McDonald also criticised shopkeepers who put odd articles such as chocolates and tins of coffee in their windows to keep the lights on.

NEW INSTRUCTIONS. Delightful stone built Cottage, believed to have been a Coach House, now converted into a high stone wall... Internal inspection strongly recommended.

The next fund raising event for the association is a Car Wash to be held on Saturday 11 June at the village hall car park starting at 10am. Refreshments will be provided to occupants of cars whilst they are being washed.

International publishing company require a keyboard operator. We are a young, efficient team... The ideal candidate will have above average keyboard skills...

22-year-old. After that spacial woman. Please write soon. Box No...

Mothers' Union Rota – to help with tease for Toddler Group on Tuesdays at 2.00pm in the Rest Centre.

In a standard wedding report form, under *Any other details or unusual features*, one couple wrote "We both turned up."

Party political candidates can be a bit of a self-promotional pain – and, occasionally, they need to be reminded of this, as in this extract from a paper's comment section.
PS: Youthful [name] *stayed at the --- Hotel in Blackpool during the Labour Party conference. I know this because he took the trouble to send this newspaper nine identical copies of a memo saying so.*

Failure to unite the correct photo and caption department

This happens more often than papers would admit, and here's just a few of them. Did the sub editor insert the wrong photo or the wrong caption? Either way, a comic mismatch ensues, to everyone's embarrassment.

Under the photo of a smiling lady leaning on a church alter with a large cross opposite her and a selection of floral decorations between the two, the caption begins: *Mrs --- judges the poultry trussing at Devon YFC County Rally...*

On a separate page, we read the caption *Mrs ---, organiser of the --- Parish Church Flower Festival, adjusts a colourful alter design.* This shows a picture of a lady and two young men staring at a low table full of plucked and trussed chickens.

A quiet, rural picture of a parish church, brushed with dappled sunlight from its leafless autumnal trees, wore the headline: *Jungle training and sub-aqua work.*

One classic example of this mismatching appeared in a local evening paper. It carried a picture of a stork landing on a rooftop nest with the headline *Helicopter's icing trials.* On a separate page of the same edition there appeared a photograph of a helicopter flying over a pine forest with the headline *Stork returns to its nest.*

A caption "Guests at the annual dinner of -- branch of the Multiple Sclerosis Society held at -- restaurant last night" was accompanied by a photograph of a man in a suit on one knee in an agricultural pen next to two pigs.

Kockout team

Illuminating remark from a Trades Council delegate: "When I say *we*, I mean *us*."

One sub-editor wrote *p... p... pick* in a headline (the reason for this cod speech impediment now escapes me), which was fortunately rescued just before publication when it was spotted that the printers had translated it into the rather unseemly *poo poo pick.*

Unfortunate headline: IT'S TREMENDOUS, SAYS AIDS SPECIALIST.

Some other intriguing headlines...

'GENTLE JERKS' TO WARM UP MEMBERS
UNWELCOME FROTH BLOWS DOWN LOVE LANE
TOWN WILL GO GAY WITH OWN CARNIVAL
CASH FROM FETE GOES THROUGH THE ROOF
NO HOME FOR HER PET TORTOISE LED WOMAN TO SMASH
STATION WINDOWS
ACCIDENT ON HER WAY TO SUICIDE BID
VANDALISM AT LEPERS WALK
NEW BODY TO RUN CEMETERY

Local Bargains. FIDELITY stereo record player with speakers, plays 45 and 33 inch records, very good condition, £15.

An advert for a spiritualist church contained a SPIRITUAL HEATING session.

A column reporting the contents of a Press release by a prospective parliamentary candidate about his party's plans for pensioners in the 1980s included this line: *We will give state pensioners free cars and electricity in the winter months...* The word *cars* should have been *gas* – and I'm not sure if the gaffe was made by the candidate or the paper. Either way, the paper should have spotted the error before scuds of over-65s started queuing up for their gratis Lada.

In a report from police warning the public not to bow to the demands of chain letters and to just "throw them away" – especially those that threatened bad luck or death – there was the self-defeating line: *The letter said that it would bring bad luck if 20 copies were posted to friends and associates...* Which was, of course, the opposite of what was meant (it should have said *good* luck).

From an arts leaflet. (As a lover *of Private Eye's Pseuds' Corner*, I adore this kind of stuff. A friend of mine similarly loves equally effusive and convoluted ramblings about scientific issues).

Each performance normally involves the collaboration of dancers and musicians moving through luminous three-dimensional musical scores, and often incorporates technical gadgetry such as spinning and swinging ghetto-blasters, projected light and moving light sources, giving the work an urban feel. Although these pieces are often carried out in galleries, some have also taken place in large urban spaces, such as:

'Mainbeam,' A Ballet for Vehicles (Gateshead multi-storey car park), for a small fleet of cars, choreographed with the aid of CB radio;

'Night in bike city' (Parker's Piece, Cambridge), for 100 choreographed cyclists riding illuminated bicycles fitted with playback cassette decks;

'Accordians Afloat,' performed on the Regent's Canal, London.

As another friend often encourages me, on reading items like this: "I feel a cartoon coming on..."

Here's part of the blurb on the back of an LP sleeve for a disk of Beethoven's 1st and 8th Symphonies, pointed out to me with great mirth by my late friend Pete Gretton. Having described the 9th as "incomparable," the writer continues...

The succession of the eight earlier symphonies shows what might be described as a great constructive curve: the two inner and the two outer pairs of works are also related by virtue of their position in the series, and one might go so far as to say that the First and Eighth Symphonies are also somehow akin as the first and last points on a line, in this case a curve of development, or as the base and highest point of a spiral, differing only as regards the level on which they exist, not in the dimension of their thematic 'wavelengths'.

Dah-dah da DAH...

Advert slogan: *SONY HP511A – The Hi-Fi that breaks records!*

Classic poor sentence construction (before subbing):
"David Mudd, MP, spoke of the role of the Opposition to bring down the present Government as quickly as possible at the annual meeting of the Falmouth and Camborne Conservative and Unionist Association on Wednesday."

Should be a long meeting...

From a parish magazine: *The sponsored silence in aid of the National Brownie Effort for the RNLI certainly proved a successful venture. For one hour, twenty Brownies were silent whilst they read, made puzzles, knitted, etc... At the end of the hour Brownies gave a huge sigh of relief and rapidly disappeared.*

POOF!

Lost a coat?

ANYONE who believes they had a coat stolen from their car in the grounds of the Penventon Hotel. Redruth. on January 5. were asked this week to contact Redruth Police where the garment is being held.

I wish the owner would hurry up and come!

Strain strain

The anti-submarine frigate HMS Dundas paid a courtesy visit to Falmouth on Friday. Her white ensign ffuttering in the chill, late-afternoon winds, her crew...

```
The Falmouth Women's Gas Federation are holding a
Continental  evening  of  Alpine  Horn  Blowing
organised by the Swiss Cheese Union.
```
    This exotic announcement actually led to me write a song.

Here's a piece from a military magazine written, alas, with much unbridled excitement and conviction, especially in the emphatic closing italics (theirs, not mine).

The Navy has taken over Britain's contribution to the Western strategic development with four massive nuclear-powered *Polaris* submarines, each of which can devastate a region 2,500 miles away. *No place on earth is more than 2,500 miles from the sea.*

From the 1815 Falmouth Guide: *Thus encouraged, Mr Killigrew went on with his erections and Falmouth started up a complete town at once.*

Reporter 1: "What's a cat o' nine tails?"
Reporter 2: "Meowww. Wag, wag, wag, wag, wag, wag, wag, wag, wag."

On coming across an advertisement for a bull hiring service called Hire-A-Sire, one office wag commented: "Perhaps hive owners in search of bees could Phone-A-Drone."

We are most fortunate in having Sister ---- as our district youth advisor and training officer. Please make use of her many talents.

The Cornwall Cadets are providing their Chaplain with some exciting and rewarding opportunities.

On a condom machine:
Manufactured to British Standard No B.S.3704
Underneath, in felt pen:
So was Titanic!

On a small patch of grass at Newquay: the notice "It is forbidden to walk, run, stand, sit or lie on the grass in this pleasure ground."

I think that's covered all bases, short of levitation.

Final paragraph from a feature on a RNAS Culdrose pilot:
He is flying again in ten hours' time, but sleep is still some way off. "I'll go home, give my wife a shake, and be full of the joys of spring!"

A plumber who was caught by police when he was urinating against a doctor's surgery wall was reported to have said: "Now you have booked me, can I finish?" --- Magistrates heard yesterday.

P claimed he got back to his own side of the road before the start of the solid white line. He accused the PC of "talking down" to him. He said the police car must have been doing 168mph to have caught up with him without overtaking the trailer, which was loaded with dung, on the bend.

From a carnival report: The shameless trollops of St Trinians were convincingly portrayed by girls of the Falmouth Youth Club.

From an annual show catalogue: The Judge may ask for milkers to be stripped for inspection if she wishes."

"Can't IMAGINE why she's not giving any Milk today!"

From a local parish magazine:
Singing Building. At one time during the reconstruction of York Minster, the pneumatic drill's staccato hammering was competing with the Minster organ while Dr Francis Jackson was practising. Dr Jackson was asked "What note is that drill playing?" At once he answered, "E Flat." Dr Jackson has since said that at that moment his "Sonata on the rebirth of a cathedral" was born.

From another parish magazine:
WHITE ELEPHANT Mrs Brown

From yet another parish magazine, in a list of parish hall events:
1500-1530 LIVING WITH AN ALCOHOLIC Joy

If incentive were needed, it should be noted that the Carn Brea Leisure Centre in August alone took £8,896 through the till and was visited by between 1,000 and 3,500 people daily. Nearly 38,000 of these were swimmers.

From a story about a local athlete:
He came back from his holiday with two gold medals for running, a silver for swimming and a bronze for the long lump.

One innovation will be a single-queuing system where customers line up behind a barrier and only move forward to the counter when a widow becomes free.

Under the heading *For Anglers*:
Don Hoyle's new fortnightly gardening column appears today on Page 19.

On Wednesday, workmen had fitted in a number of the more severe potholes.

Clergymen in Devon and Cornwall are being warned by police to watch out for an escaped Broadmoor patient weighing 18 stones who thinks he is the Messiah.
The 44-year-old Guyanian was described as almost six feet tall, of stocky build with short black curly hair, brown eyes, a beard, a scar in the middle of his forehead and no teeth. Easy to spot, then.

They live at ----- with their daughters Kathryn, aged 14, and Justine, 111...

The rapist is described as about 30 years of age, 50ft 10in tall, of stocky build with a full beard and moustache. (*I think police might spot him, even without the beard info*).

PROPOSAL 5 D.17
TO CONSTRUCT IN NEWTON ABBOT THE FOLLOWING
ROADS IN THE PLAN
(1) TO BE STARTED BEFORE 1981
      (i) *HIGHWEEK STREET IMPROVEMENT*
      (cost at November 1977 prices - £0.4m)
      A scheme to relive the severe congestion caused by the high level of traffic using the A382 which is sub-standard at this point.

She was attended by her sisters Diane and Jackie, who wore brown and cream full-length carnations and yellow dresses and carried orange freesias.

During a high summer dog show "organisers were so worried about the current heat wave that they laid on ice just in case canine temperatures soared."

This means a cheaper, faster and more effective job. Work began in July 1081 and was completed in March 1982 with the exception of landscaping works.

Due to the announcement of election day on 9th June, the "Putting Animals Into Politics" Meeting arranged for 17th June has now been cancelled.

PUBLIC NOTICES
Mrs A. Allison (9000/9041)
Notice is hereby given that an application for the above development has been submitted to the ----- District Council.

Mr P.G. was yesterday cleared of setting fire to the flat above his shop on the instructions of a Recorder at Exeter Crown Court.

GIRL GUIDES 1910-1985
This year Guides all over the world celebrate 75 years of Guiding. Guides are fun and much better than watching TV...

ACTION van – part of the Centre for Titness Promotions – re-start their Fitness Friday keep fit sessions in Totnes on May 24.

A news piece celebrated the presentation to a local engineering firm of "the prestigious British Safety Council 5-Star Health and Safety Management Award."

The story added: "The 5 Star Management Audit system is one of the most comprehensive health and safety evaluations in the world."

The accompanying picture showed two delighted members of the firm and the award's presenter. They were holding a large certificate marked with FOUR large stars.

Cartoons

Over the years I have drawn cartoons for various papers that I've worked on, mostly in a very periodic, ad-hoc way and mostly unpaid. Here's a few that made it, and a few that never got past the starting gate, either because I didn't submit them or because the particular publication of the time didn't want them.

Walker

The Ten Tors Challenge is an annual two-day trek across Dartmoor in Devon in the second week of May. It is organised by the Army with 2,400 youngsters taking on hikes of 35, 45 or 55 miles across the often desolate and rugged moorland terrain and visiting ten nominated tors along their chosen route. The teams of six must be self-sufficient, camping out overnight in all weathers under the umbrella protection of army personnel, the men and helicopters of the Royal Navy and the Dartmoor Rescue Group. There are many tales of reporters' highs and lows sustained whilst covering this event – enjoying the free Army-supplied packed lunches, taking a helicopter flight, running around frantically trying to track down teams from their paper's circulation area, getting lost – but rather too many to mention. Teams arrived back elated and/or exhausted, some teenagers sustained minor injuries and sadly there were the occasional tragedies, but mostly it was a rewarding experience.

Thinking about the effects on the body, especially for the unprepared, I did the drawing below one year...

"I told you not to go on the Ten Tors 55-mile trek.
Now how are you going to get on the school bus?!"

Eggsactly

A story about an alleged egg-painting ring led to the following cartoon.

Apparently, as I wrote at the time, some cluck was having a bit of a yolk by dyeing white eggs and passing them off as brown. The scam was revealed in an anonymous phone call to Cornwall's Weights and Measures Department from someone who had shelled out for some tasty hen fruit from his village shop only to find that that the colouring came off when the eggs were boiled in salted water and vinegar. Only it was a scam that wasn't, as no evidence of tampering with the natural colour of the eggs was found. Which was a pity, because I thought the perpetrator, now found to be non-existent, could have had the colour drained from his cheeks by a fellow "entrepreneur" wanting him to re-shade **ostrich** eggs.

"Got a proposition for you, mate..."

Pillows

Anxious to discover how many holidaymakers were using its facilities, a district council tourism sub-committee resolved "that a pillow survey be approved... and the questionnaire to be used be that approved by the Sub-Committee." Needless to say, a cartoon was drawn on the back of the council agenda...

Wet

The day the Government's specially-appointed Minister for Drought Ian Gow visited the South West to take a look at its dangerously-depleted reservoirs in August 1984 the skies opened...

Minister for Drought – South West Water Press officer – Damp trainee reporter

Trees

When the deputy editor, on the hunt for a piece to complete the page he was working on, asked one of the trainees the following question without further explanation, out of the blue, I felt a cartoon was in order.

Not pigeons again!

Here are two drawings I made on planning committee agendas during the more tedious part of the day's debates.

The first concerned an application for a rabbit breeding unit and the second was for a clay pigeon shooting range, both in the countryside.

Missing at sea pair safe

Village gets new letter box because old one was dangerous

Cheque Up

For a period my newspaper seemed inundated with requests for cheque presentation pictures, often from the same establishments and often featuring huge cheques stretching out for several feet so that the donors and the amount showed clearly and publicly.

This is all fine and worthy of mention due to the work put in by various individuals and organisations for other individuals and organisations. It's just the sheer number of big cheques begin to grate after a while with reporters anxious to highlight more portentous news items. It's just one of those things that dog local community-based newspapers.

Anyway, after a spate of these pictures a frustrated reporter sent the following spoof picture request to an equally-frustrated photographer which ended up on his notice-board.

SUBJECT: Cheque presentation to all the organisations who have presented cheques to other organisations during the year by the Organisation for Presenting Cheques to Cheque-Presenting Organisations. Also top cheque presentation body gets cheque for presenting the largest cheque. Also cheque from joint cheque presenters to Association for Presentation of Cheques for presenting a cheque to other cheque presenters.
PLACE: Our Favourite School's Cheque Presentation Dept.
DAY: Each day of every week for the next 20 years* approx.
(*As each of the cheque-presenters will be presenting cheques to each other in strict rotation, the ceremony is expected to take some time).

On one occasion a newspaper gave several hundred pounds to an appeal to fund an operation for a local child and the editor decided that he would present the cheque. When the lad and his mum turned up, all the editor could go on about was the sticking plaster on child's forehead. So he had the youngster photographed with his back to the camera so that the plaster wouldn't show – because it "didn't look nice." When he handed over the company cheque he demanded that the cheque be photographed with its back to the camera too, "to be different. We always photograph them the other way round." It looked like a blank piece of paper. One reporter commented: "All the cuckoos are not in Swiss clocks by the looks of it."

Out of the Mouths of...

Children from a Cornish junior school were given a project to create their own version of their local paper. Here are three of the stories from that project which, whilst crisp and incisive, charmingly show both a critical news sense and a complete lack of it in one breath.

BANK ROBBERY

Last night at about 12.00 the Midland Bank was robbed at St Austell. 5 million pounds was taken. It appeared to be taken by some football fans wearing red and white striped scarves and some were wearing black trousers. They came from a football match. Liverpool lost against Arsenal and a person saw the fans and said they were drunk. They broke the door down.

DEATH AT SEA

In France someone was killed in the war. He was killed on a ship. He was buried at sea. His name was Jimmy and he was a captain. In a few more minutes another man died and they had to get help from another ship.

A KENNAK MYSTERY

There has been a mysterious thing coming to Kennak in the night. Several people have been reported missing these few weeks. So if anyone sees this mysterious thing, please report it.

In the words of English novelist Dame Rose Macaulay: "You should always believe all you read in the newspapers – as that makes them more interesting."

You don't have to be mad to work elsewhere, too...

At the Literature Festival

A well-known bookstore chain ran the main book shop in a side room at a local literature festival and also organised the signing sessions in a nearby marquee. On one particular year I went into the main shop minutes after it had opened and saw a lot of feverish activity – people running in and out with boxes of books and a couple of guys setting up a computer and electric till. Then I heard the following exchange, which pretty much sums up the potty pecking levels peculiar to British industry/commerce.

Pale and lanky youth (*behind till, to next-in-line company superior, barely older than him but less pale*): "Is putting the sign up in the entrance the first priority?"

Next-in-line superior: "No. We need to get the computer up and running and the till on."

Pale: "Because I was told the sign was the number one priority."

Superior: "Who told you that?"

Pale (*referring to someone presumably ranked between Pale and his present accompanist*): "Terry."

Superior: "Well, don't take any notice of Terry. I'm telling you to get the computer and the till on. That's your number one priority. And if Terry comes back and asks you why you haven't put the sign up, tell him that I told you that the computer and the till take priority."

Pause for re-think.

Superior (*continued*): "Unless Terry comes back and tells you that Chris (*presumably a more elevated superior than Pale's next-in-line superior*) told him to tell you to put the sign up as a matter of priority. In which case, you put the sign up."

That's telling him!

At a Popular Supermarket

I was in a popular supermarket and, as I only had one item, I went to an aisle that looked like a quick escape, with only one couple being served. The woman commanding the checkout was in her late fifties/early sixties, a bit cheerless looking and very slow. She was serving a man and woman in their sixties/seventies, the man in a baseball cap and tee shirt, the woman in a holiday frock. The checkout woman began chattering away in a rather disinterested/distracted Catherine Tate kind of voice to brief replies, or none, from the two customers who clearly wanted to pack their goods and go.

"Are you local?"

No.

"On holiday, then?"

Yes.

"Where are you from?"

New Zealand.

Till lady brightens up.

"Oh, I've got a daughter in Australia!"

This, I thought, was geographically similar to telling a Londoner "I've got a relative in Dublin."

Then the man produced his credit card, American Express, to the checkout woman's response: "Oh, I've never seen one of those before. I don't know if we take them."

It was like she was being presented with a store card from an obscure videogame rental shop.

She called a supervisor, to the astounded expressions of her Antipodean customers and asked her: "If I ask them for ID can I take this?"

The supervisor told her subordinate to accept the card, the bill was paid and the foreign bodies departed, shaking their heads.

Fortunately, the only question I was asked was: "Do you have our store club card?"

"No," I said. And thought: And I don't have the kind of income that allows me to carry the internationally-renowned and prestigious American Express card, either!

Part 9

Magic Moments

Magic moments on the other side of the ribbon

Magic Moments on the Other Side of the Ribbon

Reporter (*returning from interview room*): "That was the man who was nearly struck by lightning."

Chief Reporter: "Nearly? That's not good enough."

Reporter: "Well, he was only 50 yards away..."

Chief: "But that's like saying 'I would have been in a car crash if I'd been in the road at the time.'"

Reporter: "I think there's a problem at our print works. The word polio has come out as 'police.'"

Reporter (*after telephone-interviewing a retiring vicar and repeatedly calling him 'Friar'*): "It said "Fr" in the phone book, so I took that to mean Friar. He said to me 'I'm not a fish and chip shop owner, you know...'"

Editor: "The comps are always leaving full stops off captions – and they know it's our style to finish a caption with one."

Deputy Editor: "Yes, but they keep putting full stops at the end of headlines instead, which isn't our house style."

Editor: "Perhaps we ought to encourage them to do that."

Chief Reporter: "Oh, don't suggest that. They'll be putting full stops at the beginning!"

Keen to promote anything in the small community where he lived, one editor had reporters pursuing the results of a weekend Conker Championships.

Sub-editor Tom has a puzzling query about a story he is subbing from reporter Adrian.

Tom: "Adrian, this Mr Dickie Stamps you refer to. What's his name?"

Adrian: "Mr Richard Stamps. Why?"

Tom: "Well, it changes half way through."

Reporter Teebone (*without looking up*): "He's got first and second class names..."

A press release arrived for an upcoming sporting event for people who had undergone major surgery. It was tagged *The Transplant Games*. Quoth chief reporter sickly: "I look forward to the pass-the-liver relay race..."

During his week's holiday, one subbing genius sent the office a postcard with a photo of the very town where his newspaper was based. This was a tad eccentric, but fine, and a bit of a nice in-joke. However, he had corrected a spelling error in the name of the cover scene that was printed on the back of the card and one reporter observed, stunned: "He even subs postcards!"

On another occasion the same sub sent his office a picture of his home village whilst on holiday, with the line "having wonderful time, food good, weather poor."

Reporter 1 (*coarsely*): "Is that all he thinks about, the paper, when he's giving his misses one?"

Reporter 2 (*likewise*): "He probably says something like: 'That reminds me, dear, there's a hole to fill on page five...'"

Answering a phone query

Sub-editor Tom (*reading part of a story in the evening paper*): "*When his wife died, social services gave him a telephone...*"

Edwin the Editor: That's no substitute!

Adrian (*reading aloud his longish caption for a photograph of a man in a hard hat looking out over the town from about 150ft up*): "The site foreman in charge of the work being carried out to convert the church into office accommodation said as he leant on the top rail, 'I'll never see this view of the street again in my lifetime.'"

As one, the office team added: "*And then he jumped!*"

Reporter Teebone (*to deputy editor Tom*): "Tom, what's our postcode?"

Tom silently points to a large sign on the notice board six inches behind Teebone's head which has been pinned there for months and can be read from the far side of the office.

It has the paper's postcode on it.

There was a call for Adrian that went through to Tom's phone. Tom took it and then patched it through to Adrian.

Tom: "Adrian, a Mr Kingdom for you."

Adrian: "Oh, right. Hello, Mr Kingdom... Hello? Er... There's nobody here."

Tom: "He must have rung off."

Beeno: "Well, there you are, Adrian. As the Bible says *Thy Kingdom go...*"

Editor (*sitting at his desk several days after Comic Relief, his pen poised over his expenses claim, to himself*): "I wonder if I can charge for my comic noses?"

A new advertising girl arrived early for her first day at the paper and Beeno let her in through the Editorial door because she was wandering around outside looking lost. She asked to use the loo, so Beeno took here there and afterwards escorted her down the corridor to the front office where he found receptionist Harriett removing her coat.

Beeno: "This is Brenda. She's just starting with you today."

Harriett: "Oh, hello, I'm Harriett. Do you know where the cloakroom is?"

And without waiting for an affirmative response escorted Brenda back down the corridor to the loo.

Photographer Cary Grantham rushes into editorial looking flustered.

Cary: "There's a Mrs Parsons who's been put through to me. She wants you, Beeno."

    Beeno: "Well, switch her through to me, then."

    Cary: "How do I do that?"

    Beeno (*surprised*): "Tap out my extension number, 135."

    Cary: "Oh."

    He disappears. He returns. Beeno is going "hello, hello" at nothing.

    Beeno: "There's nobody here."

    Sam: "Have you pressed the little orange button?"

    Cary: "What orange button?"

    Adrian shows him.

    Sam: "Press that first, then the extension number."

    Cary: "Oh."

    He leaves. He returns. Beeno still has no-one on the line.

    Beeno (*twigging*): "Have you put your phone down?"

    Cary: "No."

    Beeno (*exasperated*): "Well, you can't transfer the call until you do!"

    Cary: "Oh."

    Exits again.

    Beeno: "How long has he been working here?!"

Tony Sears' Subbing Question of the Week: "Whitney, you don't know the name of these two persons who took part in the egg-catching competition do you?"

Teebone: "What do you call a bear with no ear?"

    Beeno: "Dunno."

    Teebone: "B."

    Response...

    Whitney: "What do you call Postman Pat when he retires?"

    Teebone: "Dunno."

    Whitney: "Pat."

Making a splash

Sub-editor Sam often took it into his head to stride across the office with his half-empty mug of drinking water and discard its unwanted contents outside.

One day he did his usual Western lope, flung open the door and tossed the water into the great outdoors. There was an "*urgfh*" and deputy editor Tom Sears appeared, soaked all over his face and shoulders. Tom had wandered off up the corridor a few moments earlier and had decided to walk back to the newsroom around the front of the building for a breath of fresh air. As he rounded the corner by the editor's office he was hit full in the face.

The office treated the incident with due respect (uncontrollable laughter).

Whitney's Critique

Trainee Whitney (*looking at a submitted wedding photo of a ruddy-cheeked couple smiling at the camera*): "They look a bit flushed."

Beeno: "Yes."

Whitney: "He looks like a farmer."

Beeno: "So does she."

Whitney (*a little hyper-critically*): "She looks like one of the farm animals!"

Apparently on a roll, or looking for a husband, Whitney then sets about one of the local landed gentry whose picture has landed on her desk as part of a potential news item.

Whitney: "He looks a right gonk."

Sub-editor Tom (*protesting*): "He's only twenty-five."

Adrian: "He's thirty-eight."

Whitney: "Thirty-eight?!" (*The second most fearful age to that of Methuselah*).

Beeno (*remembering he's just passed forty-one*): "Life doesn't stop at 38."

Whitney: "It does when you look like that!"

To Squiff (From Whitney)

Witnessing the birth of a new descriptive word

Tom the sub (*examining a story from Whitney*): "Have you finished this?"

Trainee Whitney: "Yes. It's not very long."

Tom: "No, I don't want it very long."

Whitney: "The last paragraph is a bit squiffy."

Tom (*puzzled*): "*Squiffy*? You mean I've got to read it like this?" (*Holds story askew.*)

Whitney: "No, I mean it's not very important, and can be squiffed out."

Therefore: to *squiff* is to delete. From the popular adjective *squiffy*, meaning a tad drunk or cockeyed.

A quite acceptable new addition to the lexicon methinks.

Lesson

Adrian was asked to address an association of Community Health Councils on how to prepare information for the media. They specifically requested him because of his previous radio experience and Ed the Editor gave him the thumbs-up to attend, as it was taking place during the day.

Said Adrian, smiling: "I might learn something from it – like how to write a Press release."

Said Sam the sub (*looking skyward*): "Many a true word..."

District office reporter and outdoor girl Kerry Smile's quote of the week, whilst relating a watery tale: "I took ages to get into my wet suit the other day – and then I discovered it was inside out."

Chief photographer Roly: "I hear Tom is to have an operation on his neck."

Beeno: "Really?"

Roly: "New bolt."

Teebone (relating the problems of starting his car in the mornings): "It only happens when the weather is damp."

Whitney: "Perhaps it's got rheumatism."

Beeno: "I can see your next job will be the motoring pages, Whitney."

Teebone (*reading paper*): "There's a story here about a medical student who swallowed a load of coins. What a way to go!"

Beeno: "The hospital gave a condition check and said there was 'no change.'"

Flying Chairs

Beeno had been complaining about his office chair for some time. One of his chairs was in such a dilapidated state that he had to Sellotape a plastic bag over the seat because it was dropping bits of packing foam all over the lino flooring. Then one of the springs broke and began poking out of the centre of the seat and he had to fix some stiff cardboard over the hole to prevent being skewered in the testicles.

One day – much to Beeno's surprise, after months of requesting a replacement sit-upon – Editor Edwin arrived with a brand new chair.

Never one to view the world with a "glass half full" perspective, Beeno observed: "It's good and firm and comfortable but with very frisky casters so that every time I sneeze or try to shut a drawer I fly back three feet. I am also able to propel myself around the room like Ironside."

Hampering an Investigation

The newspaper had a break-in one weekend. When Beeno arrived, he discovered that subs Sears and Trafford were on the case when reporter Teebone looked up from his typewriter and facetiously announced: "Detective Constable Sears and Detective Sergeant Trafford are investigating."

In true Holmesian fashion, sub Tom Sears opened his top drawer delicately with his finger, then probed about inside with the tip of his letter-opener. Nothing was missing.

Sub Sam Trafford began holding his phone with a piece of copy paper between his hand and the receiver, presumably to retain any errant fingerprints, and Adrian mumbled: "That's going a bit over the top, isn't it?"

Ironically, the first Press release to emerge from the morning's post was the leaflet *Protect your Office from Crime*.

Anyway, the burglars took about £4 from the coffee machine (but wisely none of the coffee) and nothing else, breaking into the Ladies loo and leaving through the Photographic window. While Beeno interviewed the real investigating Detective Constable for details of any similar breaks that had taken place over the weekend, Editor Edwin hovered at the side adding the occasional question of his own, some of them actually pertinent.

At one point the DC indicated the outline of a footprint on one of the photographic stools saying they would have to check it out.

"Oh, that's my footprint," Edwin volunteered, to some surprise. "I got up on the stool to shut the window."

Er, the window that the robbers had opened to escape through... No tampering with a crime scene, then.

The entire staff was fingerprinted for the process of elimination, though the perpetrators were never caught.

On another occasion when there was a walk-in theft from the front office, the managing director had all the locks changed – only to leave his own keys in the front door, which were eventually retrieved by a very disgruntled locksmith.

Teebone: "I got the book of *Allo Allo* for my birthday with a cheese board and a bottle of wine."

Beeno: "That's nice."

Teebone: "Yes, I got the whole lot."

Beeno: "Nice present."

Teebone: "Yes, but I wanted Yvette."

Adrian: "I'm beginning to realise that if you can write a story straight away, it's much clearer in your mind and much easier to write. I'm learning all the time."

Beeno: "Well, that goes without saying, Adrian. The longer you leave a story, the dimmer your recollection of it gets."

Adrian: "Is that right? That's normal is it? Well, as I said, I'm always learning."

Adrian rings the daughter of a local woman for information about her mum who is about to celebrate her 100th birthday. During the course of the interview, Adrian asks: "And is she a Miss or a Mrs?"

Photographer Cary Grantham spots the editor sitting at Beeno's desk with headphones on, typing studiously and grunting from time to time. He is taking down some news copy from someone.

Cary (*entering*): "Is Edwin on the phone?"

Beeno (*facetiously*): "No, his ears were just cold."

Adrian (*to office in general*): "Where's Prague? I hope it's not in Czechoslovakia..."

Beeno: "Well, where would you like it to be?"

Adrian: "Anywhere but Czechoslovakia, as I'll have to spell it."

He takes out *The Oxford Dictionary for Writers and Editors* and begins thumbing pages.

Beeno (*after a while*): "C-Z-E-C-H..."

Adrian: "Oh, is that why I can't find it under C-H!"

Adrian (*into phone*): "Oh, hello, I'm just ringing to confirm that it will be all right to come along and photograph Mrs Brown on her 100th birthday because we just wanted to make sure that she, well, that nothing has happened to her since you rang us last week about the happy event and..."

He continues until he takes a breath – about another minute – then...

"Pardon? Oh. Oh, I'm dreadfully sorry. No, I must have put your number next to the other number and... No. I'm sorry Mr Williams, what I wanted to talk to you about was..."

Adrian (*to sub Tom*): "Can I put a number in an intro? I want to say *1,000 sheep at a sheep dipping trials*. Because you don't like figures in intros, do you?"

Tom (mystified): "I don't mind figures in intros. Do you mean *Can I start a story with a figure?*"

Adrian: "No. I just thought you didn't like figures in intros..."

Teebone (*grumpily*): "I should just put your figure in before people fall asleep!"

Editor Edwin: "I have the police on the phone. They are asking about an advert we had for a missing cufflink and want to know if it's been handed in to us. Does anyone know anything about it?"

Office consensus: "No."

Edwin: "Well, you take it Adrian."

Adrian: "Yes."

Adrian picks up phone and waits for call to be transferred.

Adrian: "Hello? You're speaking to Adrian Halter. We don't know anything about a missing cufflink. Right, thank you."

He puts phone down. There is office tittering.

Edwin: "Er, Adrian, I didn't mean that."

Adrian (*oblivious*): "Oh. Did you want a story?"

Adrian: "Do they call a mayor *councillor*?"

Beeno: "Yes. They have to be a councillor to become a Mayor of their council."

Adrian: "Oh. I thought there were circumstances where they could be a Mayor but not a councillor."

Someone was misnamed BALDCOCK instead of BALDOCK in a story. Quipped district office reporter Kerry Smile: "It rolls nicely off the tongue."

Adrian (on phone): "Ah, good morning. I expect I have missed Mr Parsons..."

Beeno: "Yes, but only by a nose."

An editor asked one of the reporters if a former reporter who had left the company rather ignominiously had moved house. She foolishly said yes, admitting that she knew something that her boss did not.

Editor: "Where's he gone?"

Reporter: "Wales, I think."

Editor: "Well, why wasn't I told?"

Reporter (*knowing the person involved had resigned after a dispute with the editor, and additionally feeling 'what's it to do with you?'*): "I didn't think you'd be interested."

Editor (*producing one of those quotes that should be enshrined*): "I always like to know what gossip is going on; I like to have the opportunity of deciding for myself whether or not I want to be told about something."

Ad manager Clarence Mildly set fire to the insides of the photocopier after putting thin, tatty copy paper into it instead of the recommended sheets in order "to save money."

An engineer was called and had to replace the entire roller as the heat sensors had snapped down and carved three parallel grooves in its skin, thus triple-scoring every copy taken. The work on the machine cost a lot more than the proper paper used to feed it.

Adrian (*to anyone is the room foolish enough to answer*): "Is there such a word as GUITARIST?"

Reporter Peter Armour (*standing in the middle of the newsroom and rustling through the new edition*): "I can't see it."

Edwin (*bursting out of his office*): "What are you looking for?"

Peter: "The local football club report."

Edwin (*officiously, and with some pride*): "Come to the font of all knowledge."

Beeno (*deflating editor ego while still typing*): "He's already been to me."

A district office received notification (a memo) that it was going to be redecorated. The news was broken by new managing director. According to the senior district reporter, the announcement was followed by "the arrival of a spotty schoolboy who said his father had told him to decorate the office. He went off and bought a cheap brush and some paint from Woolies and waded into the job." Turned out he was the managing director's son – a classic case of jobs for the boys (or boy).

Adrian (*on phone to local department store regarding an upcoming presentation to children in the toy department*): "Will any of the real Care Bears come along? (*Pause*) Oh. It will be someone in a Care Bears costume, will it? No. Oh. I didn't realise that. No, well, I haven't seen the film. No. Anyway, I'm a Flumps fan myself..."

On another occasion, Adrian was talking to the same store about a Yummi Bears competition and referred to them as "Yuppie Bears."

Yuppie bears. The bears with the shares

Editor Edwin wanted some cigars and asked Ad manager Clarence Mildly if he'd get him some while he was out for lunch. Clarence made great play of having the right amount and which jacket pocket the cash was in.

Clarence (*patting chest*): "Now, that's Edwin's pocket..."

Beeno (*relating incident later*): "Strikes me that someone who can't handle 80p for a packet of Hamlets (*for such was the price of a noxious puff back then*) shouldn't be in charge of a department dealing with thousands of pounds a week..."

Sam turned up at work after having his mouth rearranged by the dentist and sat at his desk all day, puffed up like a pregnant gerbil and making the kind of deep-throated guttural sounds that usually precede famous last words. Coincidentally, the same day Teebone arrived at work with one tooth missing. His crown had vanished into a piece of cheese the previous night while he was wining and dining a lady friend. He later observed that, at £20 for the repair job, it was the most expensive piece of cheese he'd ever eaten.

Results

It's one thing to have a major company in your circulation area, one that provides loads of local employment and undertakes both an interesting and valuable service to the world. But it's another thing entirely to be so obsessed with publicising them at every turn that you lose a more balanced perspective.

Edwin was an editor who was almost neurotically wedded to one particular firm, getting his reporters to chase everything he could discover about them (also apparently ensuring they were almost exclusively positive items), at the expense of other large companies in the area. He also ordered regular double-page features about the company's work – which were interesting on the first two occasions and thereafter, at the very least, repetitive.

One morning – as happened regularly, twice a year – the company phoned to say its half-yearly results were available for us to collect. Edwin left chief reporter Beeno an urgent note to this effect. When Beeno arrived, he read the note, sighed and called out to Edwin: "I'll get them at lunchtime, if I can."

Beeno wasn't able to do so and when he returned from a string of other assignments which had prevented this particular trip he told Edwin he would collect the results first thing in the morning. Edwin's eyes went wild; packed with that haunted look kids get just before you threaten to confiscate their Smarties to stop them spoiling their tea.

"But they may not keep them there for us," he whimpered. "They might *take them away.*"

Beeno looked at him long-sufferingly and calmly replied: "If they've taken them away, I'll ask them to *bring them back*."

The editor looked relieved and was later heard whistling (or was it just the wind in the eaves?). Beeno collected the Holy Grail the next morning, as promised, and there was joy and rejoicing in the land.

Reporter (*to telephonist, flippantly*): "I'm expecting a message from the Cornish yodelling champion."

Receptionist (*gullibly*): "Are you?"

Reporter: "Yes. If he calls would you mind opening the window?"

An A4 notice next to the coffee machine had the following graffiti added below the line ON DISCOVERY OR SUSPICION OF FIRE... *Yell Hooray! Direct petrol at base of flames and fan flames briskly.*

Receptionist Harriett: "A letter came to the office the other day addressed to me and I would love to have known what was in it."

Beeno (*puzzled*): "Sorry?"

Harriett: "Well, we aren't allowed to open any mail addressed to us. All the mail has to go to the advertisement manager to open."

Harriett (*typing*): *Tap tap DUNK!* "Oh, you can see how often I type!"

Beeno: "True."

Harriett: "Oh, now it's all crooked."

Beeno: "It must be on Company notepaper."

Harriett: "There's a Mrs Descent in the front office for a reporter."

Beeno: Right, I'll be down in a minute.

Edwin: Oh, *very* good!

Harriett (*later*): I didn't get that one.

One of the girls in advertising is leaving and looking about nineteen months pregnant.

Harriett (*walking into the news room and announcing*): "If anyone is giving anything for Tammi's farewell, could you give it to me in the next few days and not at the last minute?"

Beeno: "I suppose a packet of condoms is too late?"

The day the first Gulf War broke out, our paper decided to do its bit for the lads (and lassies) by sending editions to local service people in the region without charge, along with any messages from relatives in a special column inside.

Harriett was usually in charge of such things and when Beeno mentioned it, Harriet responded: "We're sending messages to the Gulf?"

Beeno: "That's right. They're on page two."

Harriett: "Well, who decided that?"

Beeno: "The Powers at the Top."

Harriett: "Well, nobody told me about it."

Resisting the urge to tell Harriett that there was a chain of command and she wasn't even a clasp, no matter now useful she was, Beeno added: "It was on the front page, in the piece headed *Free Newspapers*. You've just joined the newsroom's dearth of information. After all, we only heard about the 1p rise in the cover price of the paper when we read it on the front page."

Beeno (*to a disconsolate Harriett*): "You must stop being a door mat. You're the only one who can stop people pushing you around."

Harriett: "You wait til you see my New Year's resolution. There'll be no doors open before 9am, no Harriett in at 8am..."

Beeno: "I'll believe that when I see it. Things will be just the same as usual."

Harriett: "I know..."

Beeno: "Harriett, some of us are born to lead – and some of us have *Dogsbody* tattooed across our foreheads."

Adrian arrives in the office and looks surprised to see Beeno sitting at his desk. "Oh," he says. "I've just made rude gestures to someone in a car going up the road, but it couldn't have been you..."

When the editor returned from a longish bout of sick leave, the staff clapped him into the office. When he said "I'm only here for five minutes," the staff spontaneously clapped louder.

When the son of one of his business colleagues took part in the London Marathon, the editor demanded a piece for the paper for his "very creditable" performance. He came in 21,216th...

Time Shift

All the public clocks in the town were showing different times. Out of five clocks, the choices offered were 5.45, 3.54, 9.16, 2.55 and 3.10. It was up to the onlooker to determine whether it was a.m. or p.m. – a choice principally governed by the levels of daylight at the times of observation.

Some timepieces were actually broken and the owners claimed they couldn't mend them because the clocks were out of easy reach, the closest being at first floor level. So the paper started a campaign to get them fixed, which largely worked. The initial story with pictures of the five contradictory dials had the witty headline *Better ask a policeman...*

All well and good, but the problem was that the editor had been taking a disproportionate interest in any stories involving clocks, including one extraordinary timepiece assembled from the once-fashionable schoolboy construction kit Meccano.

This went on for at least a year and reached a point where some staff – mainly the chief photographer, who was often saddled with demands for more and more shots of clocks, their locations, state of repair and their owners – would often whisper *"tick tick tick..."* whenever the editor passed by, immoderately suggesting that maybe some of his boss's own internal cogs had gone a bit wonky.

And this led to the cartoon, which sort-of incorporated both sides of the argument.

"There's nothing unusual in having an interest in clocks, Roly."

The editor was away sick, but kept ringing in with story tips and queries. The final straw came when he made the umpteenth call about a power cut near his home village. Commented a disgruntled Teebone: "They'll be putting a phone in his coffin!"

Adrian was getting a bit of pressure from the editor about a story he was writing on a new college principal who was both a professor and a doctor, and the editor kept reminding Adrian of these appellations. He was eventually left to his own devices and began typing the story.

Beeno (*impishly*): "Don't forget it's Professor Doctor, Adrian."

Adrian (*sweating*): "Yes, yes. I know, I know."

Beeno: "Isn't it nice to know he's not a Councillor too?"

Adrian: "Oh, shut up."

Beeno: "Councillor Professor Doctor. Mmm, rolls nicely off the tongue, doesn't it?"

And among the additional queries requested by the editor for Adrian to ask the ProfDoc (or is is DocProf?) was: "Ask him how much he got for his house," which didn't seem all that pertinent.

Wholly

When one of the senior editorial team, a fairly committed Christian, made a trip to the Holy Land, it was decided that he should write about it. Fair enough. However, what emerged was a massive two-page spread on what was effectively a collection of holiday snaps and memories. It came at a time – which is most of the time in local newspapers – when the paper was short of space for reports on events in its own circulation area, including carnivals, fetes and so on; events with lots of local faces in the accompanying photographs, rather than two pages of sandy foreign monuments and non-local Israelis. I'm afraid the whole controversy led to the following cartoon, which I wisely did not share with the person involved.

"I can type with two hands since my trip to the Holy Land."

One reporter seemed to take an age to write his stories. It was finally discovered that he operated a two-tier system, typing at least half his pieces TWICE – "one to help me get my thoughts together and the second for the paper."

De-composing

Edwin removed the name of a composer from a piece Beeno had written about a classical guitarist that listed seven of the composers whose music the fret-teasing exponent most liked to play. The one his editor deleted was Ponce. Beeno asked why.

Edwin: "Oh, I looked him up in my encyclopaedia and a book of composers and I couldn't find his name."

Beeno: "Well, he does exist, otherwise I wouldn't have included his name."

Edwin: "Well, the list was long enough – and I'd rather be safe."

And so the lesser-known Manuel Maria Ponce (1882-1948, born Mexico City, educated Conservatorio Nacional de Musica) was consigned to remain a little more obscure than fellow guitar composition masters such as Spaniard Joaquin Rodrigo (*Concierto de Aranjuez*) and Brazilian Heitor Villa-Lobos.

Mind you, Beeno probably laid his own bed of doubt with his editor as, some months earlier, he had submitted the following spoof story (*below*), including loads of spurious statistics, and only owned up when he spotted Edwin in the middle of subbing it for a sports page.

"I thought it sounded odd," Edwin responded. "I was getting suspicious."

[*Name of town*] Ratting Club
The first rat of the season was caught at Ricklesworth Pond on Saturday by John Elmes in 2.12.22/7 with a ham and lengthlock trill and twine. Harold Evans and Charlie Curry took joint water vole and rat twinsome (6.11.31 and 8.17.20/2) with gapper hook and modified point-22.
Club secretary Jim Paver said the day's mulching was successful, with 23 fast-rat and 11 medium breeds culminated. The South and West Devon League now shows Exeter's 411 Club in prime position (631 over 12.9 in 16.5), with our club a rising 43rd in the league. Harry Carter, Press Secretary. Any more info ring Jim Paver.

Pritty Painful

Beeno borrowed Sam's large Prit stick and when he'd finished with it decided to toss it back across the office to its owner rather than exercise himself with the five foot walk between desks. Sam stood up, adopted a wicket keeper stance (being a dab hand at the game) and said "Okay!" All to no avail, as the plastic projectile went straight through his fingers and it hit him a sharp blow in the goolies. He went "Oooh" and bent double.

At this moment a pretty advertising girl walked into the office. She turned to Sam and said: "I want you to do me a favour."

She was totally confused when Beeno and Sam burst out laughing after the stooping sub wheezed his reply in a high voice: "Not at the moment!"

Remember where you are

A reporter who had to dial a nine to get an outside line on his office phone dialled a nine to get an outside line on his home phone one weekend.

Puzzled when he failed to get a dialling tone, he tried again... and again.

"Fire, police or ambulance?" came the unexpected voice in his ear.

Trainee (*on phone*): "And how was the money raised?"

Reporter next to her: "By holding it in the air."

Trainee (*on phone to athlete*): "So, you've been running for about ten years now?"

Second trainee (*nearby*): "She must be nackered!"

Trainee Whitney (in a quiet spell in the office): "How do you spell *Old MacDonald's Farm*?"

Adrian: "O. L. D... M. A. C... or is it just M. C? D. O. N... er..."

Whitney: "No, no. *E. I. E. I. O!*"

(*Thank you, Whitney!*)

Suicide – or Taking Cruel Advantage Of The Innocent (Rude)

Newly-arrived trainee Whitney Finch was studying a rival newspaper when she spotted a story of interest. But she could not understand why chief reporter Beeno and reporter Adrian began laughing when she said: "You know this suicide? He was found in his car clutching a handkerchief in his hand."

Beeno: "Really?"

Whitney: "He must have been wiping away the tears."

Beeno: "Well, he was certainly wiping away something."

Adrian: "Yes, he'd probably had his handful."

Whitney (*dawn breaking*): "Are you saying what I think you're saying?"

Beeno/Adrian (*unconvincingly*): "No..."

Whitney: "You dirty-minded buggers. I've gone all red."

Beeno: "He probably did too."

Adrian: "That's true."

Whitney: "Oh, shut up!"

Part 10
Finale

Goodbye to all that
Poem in a pot
Magical memos
And finally...

Goodbye to All That
Well, Most of it...

It was the last day in the old offices and the place had been stripped of most of the paraphernalia that had made it home for decades, albeit a rather tatty home. On the Monday we would be moving into new premises on the other side of town.

Photographer Cary brought in his video camera to capture what turned out to be around three minutes of magic moments, including the arrival of Edwin. As he opened the newsroom door, Beeno leapt in front of the editor clutching a black rolled up folding umbrella that looked like a mock microphone and asked him what he thought of the move, in true TV news style (breathless and over-eager).

"Bollocks!" said the editor, and then looked around at the denuded room with a gaze of quiet distress.

He grew slightly more distressed when he realised there was a film cassette in the camera.

His concern grew further during the morning over what was being dumped in a large yellow skip outside, which the entire staff was filling with great enthusiasm.

One of the first things to go was the half-full can of ant powder. [Actually, that sounds good in print, but I have a feeling that the ant powder, a can of fly spray and some furniture polish were left behind, abandoned on the shelf where they had lived a lifetime in product terms, clustered side-by-side like an especially ugly collection of cylindrical aluminium tea caddies.]

When Beeno and Whitney left for lunch at 1pm, the former looked at the skip and said: "He'll probably be rummaging around in that while we're out." He was.

On their return they found an old glass ashtray, previously used by a reporter who had left the company months earlier, had been retrieved by Edwin "because it might be worth something" (it wasn't) along with a rusted metal helical pencil sharpener with an eight hole selector of different-sized apertures and a cranking handle, a rarely-used but still functional item that was formerly screwed to a shelf over one of the night store heaters. It made its way up to the new offices but was never screwed to anything again and spent its final days as a begrimed grey ornament on the editor's new desk.

Staff were told that there would be NO posters on the walls of the new offices and all desks would have place mats to prevent coffee stains smearing the new furniture.

Quoteth Whitney: "This company doesn't half go to extremes. One minute we're working in a pig sty with tatty old furniture and the next we're getting place mats!"

Happy memories...

Poem in a Pot

In (almost) closing, I have reproduced a poem from a 1925 broadsheet, from a time when newspapers delighted in publishing readers' submitted verses.

Finding florid little gems like this is one of the delights of paging back through old editions of newspapers – bound in stiff cardboard sleeves, their pages yellowed, brittle and smelling of desiccation dust, long-gone days and (depending on how well the volumes are stored) mouse droppings.

Unsurprisingly, it still has a message for us today.

Vegetation

Give me the life which moves along
In unabashed audacity,
A merry life of wine and song,
Enlivened by loquacity.

II
I seek not power, or place, or pelf*
If there entail duplicity;
But quite refuse to clothe myself
In vacuous simplicity.

III
I do not care to imitate
In somnolent tranquillity
The ways of those who rusticate
In otiose docility.

IV
Who strive their lives to consecrate
With half-concealed facility
To all they claim to abrogate
In ill-assumed humility.

V

They never can appreciate
Existence in totality,
Who only seek to re-create
Traditional morality.

VI

I much prefer to cultivate
A talent for publicity,
Than cabbage like to vegetate
In fatuous rusticity.

E. POWELL

Note: "pelf" is archaic for money gained dishonourably

The Magical Memos of those to whom this book is dedicated

1

Lance came up with some great memos, often using official, printed company memorandums headed with his name and title in the manner that all such forms should be used – instructionally, yet informally and with an air of mischief.

On one occasion he wrote: *That was a good workmanlike job you did on the Ten Tors expedition. But I'm sure you're pulling my leg when you repeatedly write GRAMMAR School with an "E."*

Still, my favourite memo is one that appeared in front of me one morning when I was being particularly effusive:

To: BRIAN THOMAS

From Lance Samson, Editor.

HUSH!

2

Noel often bashed out a memo to give instructions to his chosen reporter on coverage of a potential story.

It was always in his inimitable, witty style.

One of my favourites was the following.

```
Brian:

Jolly Tales Dept.                    Abraham and the Jewish hordes.

Lambs Lane (the access road to       I would think people living there

Ashfield Estate, or one of the      are BRAHNED ORFF to put it

access roads, anyway). Council       mildly. Please investigate.

workmen have been widening this      I think some of the council men

road now for a generation or two.    have decided to make a career out

Before work started, haggling        of the job.

went on, dating back to                        Noel 24.iv
```

3

Sue was always a great laugh and has remained a valued friend ever since she was a trainee back in the 1980s. Her greatest "memo" came about like this.

Most reporters have nick-names for some of their more notable contacts, mostly benign parodies based on their looks or mannerisms.

One of the paper's frequent correspondents looked a little (OK, a lot) like the famous spinach-eating cartoon sailor, and acquired the appropriate, unkind nick-name.

One day I was busy on the phone when Sue, anxious to attract my attention shoved a piece of copy paper and its illustration below under my nose, which included the (here-deleted) phone number.

Needless to say, I snorted with laughter into the phone (to the consternation of the person on the other end who thought my reaction was aimed at them).

Nice one, Sue!

4

Mike, to be honest, has never sent me a memo as we never actually worked in the same office together. But he has sent me swathes of emails and loads of letters over the many years we have been colleagues and friends.

A favourite email (of course) relates to the very book you are holding, after I gave him a copy of the opening chapter.

I couldn't have wished for a better recommendation – from a career journalist and writer who has tackled most subjects but is especially adept at evoking his home town, the Cornish port of Falmouth, and the many tales of its vibrant waters (check out his book *Reflections*, which he kindly asked me to illustrate, available from his local Cancer Research shop).

He wrote:

Devoured every word of The Other Side of the Ribbon *last night. Had it in mind just to begin it over tea, but I was so totally hooked on it I just couldn't stop... Entertainment-wise, it should be "required reading" for journalists, past and present, everywhere, and a whole lot more people besides.*

What more can I say, dear reader?

Except...

Thank you for wending your way to the end of this little diversion. I hope it made you laugh and brightened your day.

Brian Thomas,
April 2016

And finally...

Adrian

Do you know they pay £100 for a funny story in the *Readers Digest*?

Tom

I can never think of anything to send them, because they've got to be true stories.

Beeno

There's a wealth of them here.

Adrian

Yes, there are hundreds of true stories at this paper you could do.

And these were just some of them...

By the author of

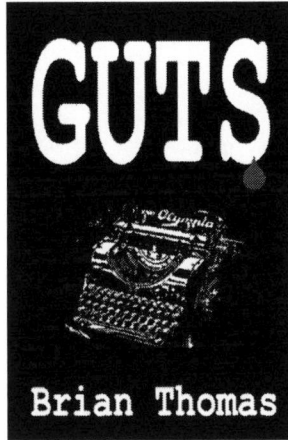

From Amazon or CreateSpace

Printed in Poland
by Amazon Fulfillment
Poland Sp. z o.o., Wrocław